Introduction

Welcome to the world of Instant Pot cooking! This cookbook is a collection of delicious and diverse recipes specifically designed for your Instant Pot. Whether you're a seasoned Instant Pot enthusiast or just starting out, this cookbook will guide you through a culinary journey filled with convenience, flavor, and creativity.

Inside these pages, you'll find a wide range of recipes that showcase the incredible versatility of the Instant Pot. From quick and easy weeknight meals to indulgent desserts, from hearty soups to mouthwatering main dishes, this cookbook has something for everyone.

With the Instant Pot, you can say goodbye to long hours spent in the kitchen and hello to effortless cooking. It's a multi-functional kitchen appliance that combines the functions of a pressure cooker, slow cooker, rice cooker, steamer, sauté pan, and more. This means you can whip up a delicious meal in a fraction of the time it would take using traditional cooking methods.

Not only does the Instant Pot save you time, but it also preserves the flavors and nutrients of your ingredients, resulting in perfectly cooked meals every time. Plus, its sealed and pressurized cooking environment locks in moisture, ensuring that your dishes are moist, tender, and bursting with flavor.

In this cookbook, you'll discover a wide variety of recipes that cater to different tastes and dietary preferences. Whether you're looking for healthy and nourishing options, family-friendly meals, vegetarian or vegan dishes, or decadent treats, we've got you covered. Each recipe is carefully crafted with clear instructions, helpful tips, and ingredient substitutions, so you can customize them to suit your preferences.

So, dust off your Instant Pot, gather your ingredients, and embark on a culinary adventure with these mouthwatering recipes. Get ready to transform your cooking experience and delight your taste buds with the ease and convenience of the Instant Pot. Let this cookbook be your trusted companion as you explore the endless possibilities that await you in the world of Instant Pot cooking. Happy cooking!

Instant Pot Cheesecake

Ingredients:

2 cups graham cracker crumbs
1/2 cup unsalted butter, melted
2 (8-ounce) packages cream cheese, softened
1/2 cup granulated sugar
2 tablespoons all-purpose flour
1 teaspoon vanilla extract
2 large eggs
1/2 cup sour cream

For the topping:

1 cup sour cream
2 tablespoons granulated sugar
1/2 teaspoon vanilla extract

Instructions:

In a medium bowl, combine the graham cracker crumbs and melted butter until the crumbs are evenly moistened. Press the mixture into the bottom of a 7-inch springform pan, creating an even crust. Place the pan in the freezer while you prepare the filling.

In a large mixing bowl, beat the cream cheese, sugar, flour, and vanilla extract until smooth and creamy. Add the eggs, one at a time, mixing well after each addition. Finally, mix in the sour cream until well combined.

Remove the springform pan from the freezer and pour the cream cheese mixture over the crust, spreading it evenly.

Prepare the Instant Pot by adding 1 cup of water to the inner pot. Place a trivet or a heatproof sling in the pot.

Carefully lower the filled springform pan onto the trivet/sling. Close the Instant Pot lid and set the valve to the sealing position.

Select the "Manual" or "Pressure Cook" setting and set the cooking time to 30 minutes on high pressure.

Once the cooking time is complete, allow a natural pressure release for 10 minutes, then manually release any remaining pressure.

Carefully remove the cheesecake from the Instant Pot and let it cool on a wire rack for about 1 hour. Then refrigerate for at least 4 hours, preferably overnight.

For the topping, in a small bowl, whisk together the sour cream, sugar, and vanilla extract. Spread the mixture over the chilled cheesecake.

Return the cheesecake to the refrigerator for another 1-2 hours to allow the topping to set.

When ready to serve, carefully remove the sides of the springform pan. Slice the cheesecake and enjoy!

Note: You can customize the cheesecake by adding fruit toppings, caramel sauce, or chocolate ganache if desired.

Instant Pot BBQ Ribs

Ingredients:

2 racks of baby back ribs
1 cup water
1 cup BBQ sauce
1/4 cup brown sugar
2 teaspoons paprika
1 teaspoon garlic powder
1 teaspoon onion powder
1 teaspoon salt
1/2 teaspoon black pepper

Instructions:

Start by removing the membrane from the back of the ribs. This will help the flavors penetrate better. You can use a paper towel to grip the membrane and peel it off.
In a small bowl, combine the brown sugar, paprika, garlic powder, onion powder, salt, and black pepper to make a dry rub.
Rub the dry rub mixture all over the ribs, making sure to coat both sides evenly.
Pour 1 cup of water into the Instant Pot insert. Place the trivet in the pot.
Cut the racks of ribs into sections that will fit inside the Instant Pot vertically, standing on their edges. Stack the ribs on the trivet.
Close the Instant Pot lid and set the valve to the sealing position.
Select the "Manual" or "Pressure Cook" setting and set the cooking time to 25 minutes on high pressure.
Once the cooking time is complete, allow a natural pressure release for 10 minutes, then manually release any remaining pressure.
Preheat your oven to broil.
Carefully transfer the ribs to a baking sheet lined with aluminum foil.
Brush the BBQ sauce generously over the ribs, coating them on both sides.
Place the ribs under the broiler for 3-5 minutes, or until the sauce begins to caramelize and glaze the ribs. Keep a close eye on them to prevent burning.
Remove the ribs from the oven and let them rest for a few minutes.
Cut the ribs into individual servings and serve them with additional BBQ sauce on the side.
These Instant Pot BBQ ribs are tender, flavorful, and perfect for a delicious meal!

Instant Pot Lasagna

Ingredients:

1 pound ground beef
1/2 cup diced onion
3 cloves garlic, minced
9 lasagna noodles, uncooked
2 cups marinara sauce
2 cups water
1 teaspoon dried basil
1 teaspoon dried oregano
1/2 teaspoon salt
1/4 teaspoon black pepper
2 cups shredded mozzarella cheese
1/2 cup grated Parmesan cheese
Fresh basil leaves, for garnish (optional)

Instructions:

Set your Instant Pot to "Sauté" mode and add the ground beef. Cook until browned, breaking it up with a spoon as it cooks.
Add the diced onion and minced garlic to the Instant Pot and sauté for an additional 2-3 minutes, until the onions are translucent.
Press "Cancel" to turn off the sauté function. Drain any excess fat from the Instant Pot.
Break the lasagna noodles in half and arrange them over the meat mixture in a crisscross pattern, covering as much of the mixture as possible.
In a medium bowl, mix together the marinara sauce, water, dried basil, dried oregano, salt, and black pepper.
Pour this sauce mixture over the lasagna noodles, making sure to cover them completely.
Close the Instant Pot lid and set the valve to the sealing position.
Select the "Manual" or "Pressure Cook" setting and set the cooking time to 20 minutes on high pressure.
Once the cooking time is complete, allow a natural pressure release for 10 minutes, then manually release any remaining pressure.
Carefully open the Instant Pot and sprinkle the shredded mozzarella cheese and grated Parmesan cheese evenly over the lasagna.
Place the lid back on the Instant Pot and let it sit for a few minutes, allowing the residual heat to melt the cheese.
Remove the lid and garnish with fresh basil leaves if desired.
Cut into servings and serve the Instant Pot lasagna hot.
Enjoy this easy and delicious Instant Pot lasagna with your family and friends!

Instant Pot Chicken Breast

Ingredients:

2-4 boneless, skinless chicken breasts
1 cup chicken broth or water
1 teaspoon dried herbs of your choice (such as thyme, rosemary, or Italian seasoning)
1/2 teaspoon garlic powder
1/2 teaspoon onion powder
1/2 teaspoon paprika
Salt and pepper to taste

Instructions:

Season the chicken breasts with salt, pepper, garlic powder, onion powder, and paprika on both sides.
Pour the chicken broth or water into the Instant Pot.
Place the trivet in the Instant Pot and arrange the seasoned chicken breasts on top of it.
Sprinkle the dried herbs over the chicken breasts.
Close the Instant Pot lid and set the valve to the sealing position.
Select the "Manual" or "Pressure Cook" setting and set the cooking time to 8 minutes on high pressure for fresh chicken breasts. If using frozen chicken breasts, set the cooking time to 12 minutes.
Once the cooking time is complete, allow a natural pressure release for 5 minutes, then manually release any remaining pressure.
Carefully open the Instant Pot lid and use a meat thermometer to ensure the internal temperature of the chicken breasts reaches 165°F (74°C).
Remove the chicken breasts from the Instant Pot and let them rest for a few minutes before slicing or serving.
Serve the Instant Pot chicken breasts with your favorite side dishes or use them in salads, sandwiches, or ther recipes.
Note: Cooking times may vary depending on the thickness and size of the chicken breasts. Adjust the cooking time accordingly if using larger or smaller chicken breasts.

Instant Pot Roast Beef

Ingredients:

3-4 pounds beef roast (such as chuck roast or bottom round)
1 tablespoon vegetable oil
1 onion, thinly sliced
4 cloves garlic, minced
1 cup beef broth
1/4 cup soy sauce
2 tablespoons Worcestershire sauce
2 teaspoons dried thyme
2 teaspoons dried rosemary
1 teaspoon salt
1/2 teaspoon black pepper
1 tablespoon cornstarch (optional, for thickening)

Instructions:

Set your Instant Pot to "Sauté" mode and add the vegetable oil. Heat the oil until shimmering.
Season the beef roast with salt and pepper on all sides.
Place the seasoned roast in the Instant Pot and sear it on all sides until browned, about 3-4 minutes per side. This step adds flavor and helps seal in the juices.
Remove the roast from the Instant Pot and set it aside on a plate.
Add the sliced onion and minced garlic to the Instant Pot and sauté for 2-3 minutes until they start to soften.
Pour in the beef broth, soy sauce, Worcestershire sauce, dried thyme, and dried rosemary. Stir to combine.
Return the seared beef roast to the Instant Pot, placing it on top of the onions and garlic.
Close the Instant Pot lid and set the valve to the sealing position.
Select the "Manual" or "Pressure Cook" setting and set the cooking time to 60-70 minutes on high pressure, depending on the size and desired tenderness of the roast. For medium-rare, cook for 60 minutes; for medium, cook for 65-70 minutes.
Once the cooking time is complete, allow a natural pressure release for 15-20 minutes, then manually release any remaining pressure.
Carefully open the Instant Pot lid and transfer the roast to a cutting board. Let it rest for a few minutes before slicing.
If desired, you can thicken the cooking liquid into a gravy. Set the Instant Pot to "Sauté" mode again. In a small bowl, whisk together the cornstarch with a tablespoon of cold water to create a slurry. Stir the slurry into the cooking liquid in the Instant Pot and let it simmer for a few minutes until thickened.
Slice the roast beef against the grain and serve it with the gravy.
Enjoy tender and flavorful Instant Pot roast beef with your favorite side dishes!

Instant Pot Beef Stew

Ingredients:

2 pounds beef stew meat, cut into cubes
2 tablespoons flour
1 teaspoon salt
1/2 teaspoon black pepper
2 tablespoons vegetable oil
1 onion, chopped
3 cloves garlic, minced
4 carrots, peeled and sliced into chunks
3 potatoes, peeled and cubed
2 celery stalks, sliced
2 cups beef broth
1 cup red wine (optional)
2 tablespoons tomato paste
2 teaspoons Worcestershire sauce
1 teaspoon dried thyme
1 bay leaf
Chopped fresh parsley, for garnish (optional)

Instructions:

In a bowl, combine the flour, salt, and black pepper. Toss the beef stew meat in the flour mixture until coated. Set your Instant Pot to "Sauté" mode and add the vegetable oil. Once the oil is hot, add the coated beef stew meat in batches and brown it on all sides. Remove the browned meat from the Instant Pot and set it aside. Add the chopped onion to the Instant Pot and sauté for 2-3 minutes until it becomes translucent. Add the minced garlic and sauté for another 1 minute.
Add the carrots, potatoes, and celery to the Instant Pot and stir to combine with the onions and garlic.
Return the browned beef stew meat to the Instant Pot, placing it on top of the vegetables.
In a separate bowl, whisk together the beef broth, red wine (if using), tomato paste, Worcestershire sauce, dried thyme, and bay leaf. Pour this mixture over the meat and vegetables in the Instant Pot.
Close the Instant Pot lid and set the valve to the sealing position.
Select the "Manual" or "Pressure Cook" setting and set the cooking time to 35 minutes on high pressure.
Once the cooking time is complete, allow a natural pressure release for 10 minutes, then manually release any remaining pressure.
Carefully open the Instant Pot lid and remove the bay leaf. Give the stew a stir and adjust the seasoning if needed.
Ladle the beef stew into bowls and garnish with chopped fresh parsley, if desired.
Serve the delicious Instant Pot beef stew hot with crusty bread or rice for a satisfying meal. Enjoy!

Instant Pot Mac and Cheese

Ingredients:

16 ounces elbow macaroni
4 cups water
2 tablespoons butter
1 teaspoon salt
1/2 teaspoon garlic powder
1/2 teaspoon onion powder
1/4 teaspoon black pepper
2 cups shredded cheddar cheese
1 cup shredded mozzarella cheese
1/2 cup grated Parmesan cheese
1 cup milk (whole milk or 2%)
Optional toppings: chopped fresh parsley, crispy bacon, or breadcrumbs

Instructions:

Place the elbow macaroni, water, butter, salt, garlic powder, onion powder, and black pepper in the Instant Pot.
Close the Instant Pot lid and set the valve to the sealing position.
Select the "Manual" or "Pressure Cook" setting and set the cooking time to half of the time indicated on the macaroni package instructions (e.g., if the package says to cook for 8 minutes, set the Instant Pot to 4 minutes).
Once the cooking time is complete, perform a quick pressure release by carefully turning the valve to the venting position.
Carefully open the Instant Pot lid and stir the macaroni to ensure it is cooked evenly and not stuck together.
Switch the Instant Pot to "Sauté" mode and add the shredded cheddar cheese, shredded mozzarella cheese, grated Parmesan cheese, and milk. Stir continuously until the cheeses are melted and the sauce is creamy.
If desired, add any optional toppings such as chopped fresh parsley, crispy bacon, or breadcrumbs for added flavor and texture.
Serve the Instant Pot mac and cheese immediately while it's hot and creamy.
Enjoy the delicious and comforting Instant Pot mac and cheese!

Instant Pot Rice

Ingredients:

2 cups rice (white rice, basmati rice, or jasmine rice)
2 cups water or broth
1 teaspoon salt (optional)

Instructions:

Rinse the rice in a fine-mesh strainer until the water runs clear. This helps remove excess starch from the rice.
Place the rinsed rice in the Instant Pot insert.
Add water or broth to the Instant Pot. The general rule of thumb is to use a 1:1 ratio of rice to liquid for white rice, or a 1:1.25 ratio for basmati or jasmine rice. If desired, add salt for seasoning.
Stir the rice and liquid together to ensure even distribution.
Close the Instant Pot lid and set the valve to the sealing position.
Select the "Manual" or "Pressure Cook" setting and set the cooking time according to the type of rice:
For white rice: Set the cooking time to 3-5 minutes on high pressure.
For basmati or jasmine rice: Set the cooking time to 4-6 minutes on high pressure.
Once the cooking time is complete, allow a natural pressure release for 10 minutes, then manually release any remaining pressure.
Carefully open the Instant Pot lid and fluff the rice with a fork to separate the grains.
Let the rice sit for a few minutes to steam and further dry out, if desired.
Serve the Instant Pot rice as a side dish or as a base for other dishes.
Note: The cooking times may vary depending on the type of rice and personal preference. Adjust the cooking time accordingly for softer or firmer rice.

Instant Pot BBQ Pulled Pork

Ingredients:

3-4 pounds pork shoulder or pork butt, trimmed of excess fat
1 tablespoon vegetable oil
1 onion, sliced
3 cloves garlic, minced
1 cup chicken broth
1 cup BBQ sauce
1/4 cup brown sugar
2 tablespoons apple cider vinegar
1 tablespoon Worcestershire sauce
1 teaspoon smoked paprika
1 teaspoon salt
1/2 teaspoon black pepper
Hamburger buns or rolls, for serving

Instructions:

Set your Instant Pot to "Sauté" mode and add the vegetable oil. Heat the oil until shimmering.
Season the pork shoulder or pork butt with salt and black pepper on all sides.
Place the seasoned pork in the Instant Pot and sear it on all sides until browned. This step adds flavor and helps seal in the juices.
Remove the pork from the Instant Pot and set it aside on a plate.
Add the sliced onion and minced garlic to the Instant Pot and sauté for 2-3 minutes until the onions start to soften.
Pour in the chicken broth and deglaze the bottom of the pot, scraping up any browned bits.
In a separate bowl, whisk together the BBQ sauce, brown sugar, apple cider vinegar, Worcestershire sauce, smoked paprika, salt, and black pepper.
Return the seared pork to the Instant Pot, pouring the BBQ sauce mixture over the pork.
Close the Instant Pot lid and set the valve to the sealing position.
Select the "Manual" or "Pressure Cook" setting and set the cooking time to 75-90 minutes on high pressure, depending on the size and tenderness of the pork.
Once the cooking time is complete, allow a natural pressure release for 10 minutes, then manually release any remaining pressure.
Carefully open the Instant Pot lid and use two forks to shred the pork directly in the pot. The meat should be tender and easily pulled apart.
Serve the BBQ pulled pork on hamburger buns or rolls. You can spoon some of the cooking liquid from the Instant Pot over the pulled pork for added flavor and moisture.
Enjoy the delicious and tender Instant Pot BBQ pulled pork sandwiches!

Instant Pot Spaghetti

Ingredients:

1 pound ground beef
1 onion, chopped
3 cloves garlic, minced
8 ounces spaghetti noodles
24 ounces marinara sauce
2 cups water
1 teaspoon dried basil
1 teaspoon dried oregano
1/2 teaspoon salt
1/4 teaspoon black pepper
Grated Parmesan cheese, for serving
Chopped fresh parsley, for garnish (optional

Instructions:

Set your Instant Pot to "Sauté" mode and add the ground beef. Cook until browned, breaking it up with a spoon as it cooks.
Add the chopped onion and minced garlic to the Instant Pot and sauté for an additional 2-3 minutes, until the onions are translucent.
Press "Cancel" to turn off the sauté function. Drain any excess fat from the Instant Pot.
Break the spaghetti noodles in half and arrange them in a crisscross pattern over the meat mixture in the Instant Pot.
In a bowl, mix together the marinara sauce, water, dried basil, dried oregano, salt, and black pepper. Pour this sauce mixture over the spaghetti noodles, making sure to cover them completely.
Gently press down on the spaghetti noodles with a spoon to ensure they are submerged in the sauce.
Close the Instant Pot lid and set the valve to the sealing position.
Select the "Manual" or "Pressure Cook" setting and set the cooking time to half the time indicated on the spaghetti package instructions (e.g., if the package says to cook for 10 minutes, set the Instant Pot to 5 minutes).
Once the cooking time is complete, allow a natural pressure release for 5 minutes, then manually release any remaining pressure.
Carefully open the Instant Pot lid and give the spaghetti a good stir to combine the noodles with the sauce.
Serve the Instant Pot spaghetti in bowls, topping with grated Parmesan cheese and chopped fresh parsley if desired.
Enjoy the easy and flavorful Instant Pot spaghetti!

Instant Pot Hard Boiled Eggs

Ingredients:

Eggs (as many as desired)
1 cup water

Instructions:

Place the metal trivet or a steamer basket in the Instant Pot insert.
Pour 1 cup of water into the Instant Pot.
Carefully place the eggs on the trivet or in the steamer basket, making sure they are not touching the water.
Close the Instant Pot lid and set the valve to the sealing position.
Select the "Manual" or "Pressure Cook" setting and set the cooking time according to your preferred level of doneness:
5 minutes for soft-boiled eggs
6 minutes for slightly soft-centered eggs
7 minutes for creamy, custardy yolks
8 minutes for traditional hard-boiled eggs
Once the cooking time is complete, perform a quick pressure release by carefully turning the valve to the venting position.
Carefully open the Instant Pot lid and transfer the eggs to a bowl of ice water to cool and stop the cooking process.
Let the eggs sit in the ice water for about 5 minutes to ensure they are fully cooled.
Gently tap each egg on a hard surface and peel off the shell. The shells should come off easily.
Rinse the peeled eggs under cold water to remove any remaining shell pieces.
Use the hard-boiled eggs immediately or store them in the refrigerator for future use.
Enjoy your perfectly cooked Instant Pot hard-boiled eggs!

Instant Pot Pork Chops

Ingredients:

4 boneless pork chops (about 1 inch thick)
1 teaspoon paprika
1 teaspoon garlic powder
1 teaspoon dried thyme
1/2 teaspoon salt
1/4 teaspoon black pepper
2 tablespoons vegetable oil
1 cup chicken broth
1 tablespoon Worcestershire sauce
1 tablespoon Dijon mustard
2 tablespoons cornstarch (optional, for thickening)

Instructions:

In a small bowl, mix together the paprika, garlic powder, dried thyme, salt, and black pepper.
Season both sides of the pork chops with the spice mixture, rubbing it into the meat.
Set your Instant Pot to "Sauté" mode and add the vegetable oil. Heat the oil until shimmering.
Place the seasoned pork chops in the Instant Pot and sear them on both sides until browned, about 2-3 minutes per side. This step adds flavor and helps seal in the juices.
Remove the pork chops from the Instant Pot and set them aside on a plate.
Add the chicken broth, Worcestershire sauce, and Dijon mustard to the Instant Pot. Stir well to combine and scrape up any browned bits from the bottom of the pot.
Return the seared pork chops to the Instant Pot, submerging them in the liquid.
Close the Instant Pot lid and set the valve to the sealing position.
Select the "Manual" or "Pressure Cook" setting and set the cooking time to 8 minutes on high pressure.
Once the cooking time is complete, allow a natural pressure release for 5 minutes, then manually release any remaining pressure.
Carefully open the Instant Pot lid and transfer the pork chops to a serving plate.
If desired, you can thicken the cooking liquid into a gravy. Set the Instant Pot to "Sauté" mode again. In a small bowl, whisk together the cornstarch with a tablespoon of cold water to create a slurry. Stir the slurry into the cooking liquid in the Instant Pot and let it simmer for a few minutes until thickened.
Pour the gravy over the pork chops or serve it on the side.
Enjoy the tender and flavorful Instant Pot pork chops with your favorite side dishes!

Instant Pot Pork Roast

Ingredients:

3-4 pound pork shoulder or pork loin roast
1 tablespoon vegetable oil
1 onion, sliced
4 cloves garlic, minced
1 cup chicken broth or stock
1/4 cup soy sauce
2 tablespoons Worcestershire sauce
2 tablespoons brown sugar
1 tablespoon Dijon mustard
1 teaspoon dried thyme
1 teaspoon dried rosemary
1/2 teaspoon salt
1/4 teaspoon black pepper

Instructions:

Set your Instant Pot to "Sauté" mode and add the vegetable oil. Heat the oil until shimmering.
Season the pork roast with salt and black pepper on all sides.
Place the seasoned pork roast in the Instant Pot and sear it on all sides until browned. This step adds flavor and helps seal in the juices.
Remove the pork roast from the Instant Pot and set it aside on a plate.
Add the sliced onion and minced garlic to the Instant Pot and sauté for 2-3 minutes until the onions start to soften.
Pour in the chicken broth, soy sauce, Worcestershire sauce, brown sugar, Dijon mustard, dried thyme, and dried rosemary. Stir well to combine.
Return the seared pork roast to the Instant Pot, placing it on top of the onion and liquid mixture.
Close the Instant Pot lid and set the valve to the sealing position.
Select the "Manual" or "Pressure Cook" setting and set the cooking time to 60-70 minutes on high pressure, depending on the size and tenderness of the pork roast.
Once the cooking time is complete, allow a natural pressure release for 10 minutes, then manually release any remaining pressure.
Carefully open the Instant Pot lid and transfer the pork roast to a cutting board.
Let the pork roast rest for a few minutes, then slice or shred it as desired.
Serve the Instant Pot pork roast with the cooked onions and the flavorful cooking liquid as a gravy.
Enjoy the juicy and tender Instant Pot pork roast with your favorite side dishes!

Instant Pot Yogurt

Making yogurt in the Instant Pot is a simple process. Here's a recipe for Instant Pot yogurt:

Ingredients:

1 gallon (3.8 liters) milk (any percentage of fat can be used)
1/4 cup plain yogurt with live and active cultures (as a starter)

Instructions:

Pour the milk into the Instant Pot insert.

Close the Instant Pot lid and set the valve to the sealing position.
Select the "Yogurt" function on the Instant Pot. Depending on your model, you may need to press the "Adjust" button until the display shows "Boil" or "Boil Milk."
The Instant Pot will heat the milk to a temperature of around 180°F (82°C). This process helps to kill any existing bacteria and create the right environment for the yogurt cultures to grow.
Once the boiling process is complete, the Instant Pot will beep. Open the lid and let the milk cool down to around 110°F (43°C). You can speed up the cooling process by placing the insert in a water bath or using an ice bath.
Once the milk reaches the desired temperature, add the 1/4 cup of plain yogurt with live and active cultures to the milk. Stir gently to incorporate the yogurt into the milk.
Close the Instant Pot lid again and select the "Yogurt" function. This time, you'll need to adjust the time to 8-12 hours. The longer the fermentation time, the tangier the yogurt will become.
After the fermentation period, carefully remove the Instant Pot insert from the appliance and refrigerate it for at least 4 hours or overnight to allow the yogurt to set.
Once chilled, the yogurt is ready to be enjoyed. You can serve it as is or sweeten and flavor it to your preference.
Note: Remember to reserve a portion of the yogurt as a starter for your next batch. This will ensure you always have a fresh batch of homemade yogurt.
Enjoy your homemade Instant Pot yogurt!

Instant Pot Pho

Pho is a traditional Vietnamese noodle soup that typically requires long hours of simmering to develop its rich flavors. While using the Instant Pot can significantly reduce the cooking time, note that the flavors may not be as deeply infused as with the traditional method. Here's a simplified recipe for Instant Pot Pho:

Ingredients:

1 onion, halved
2-inch piece of ginger, sliced
4-5 star anise pods
2 cinnamon sticks
4-5 cloves
4 cups beef broth
4 cups water
1-2 tablespoons fish sauce
1 teaspoon sugar
8 ounces rice noodles
8 ounces beef (sliced or thinly shaved)
Bean sprouts, Thai basil, lime wedges, and sliced chili peppers for serving

Optional toppings:

Sliced green onions
Cilantro leaves
Hoisin sauce
Sriracha sauce

Instructions:

Set your Instant Pot to "Sauté" mode and add the onion halves and ginger slices. Cook for a few minutes until they start to brown and release their aromas.

Add the star anise, cinnamon sticks, and cloves to the Instant Pot. Continue sautéing for another minute to toast the spices.
Pour in the beef broth and water, followed by the fish sauce and sugar. Stir to combine.
Close the Instant Pot lid and set the valve to the sealing position.
Select the "Soup" or "Pressure Cook" setting and set the cooking time to 20 minutes on high pressure.
While the broth is cooking, prepare the rice noodles according to the package instructions. Drain and set aside.
Once the cooking time is complete, allow a natural pressure release for 10 minutes, then manually release any remaining pressure.
Carefully open the Instant Pot lid and strain the broth through a fine-mesh sieve to remove the solids.
Taste the broth and adjust the seasoning with additional fish sauce or sugar, if desired.
To serve, divide the cooked rice noodles among bowls. Top with the beef slices.
Ladle the hot broth over the noodles and beef, ensuring they are submerged.
Serve the Instant Pot Pho with a plate of bean sprouts, Thai basil, lime wedges, sliced chili peppers, and any other desired toppings.
Each person can customize their Pho by adding the toppings of their choice and squeezing lime juice into their bowl.
Enjoy your flavorful Instant Pot Pho!

Instant Pot Whole Chicken

Ingredients:

1 whole chicken (3-4 pounds)
1 tablespoon vegetable oil
1 teaspoon salt
1/2 teaspoon black pepper
1 teaspoon dried thyme
1 teaspoon paprika
1 teaspoon garlic powder
1 cup chicken broth or stock
1 lemon, sliced
Fresh herbs (such as rosemary or thyme) for garnish (optional)

Instructions:

Remove the giblets from the chicken cavity, if included, and pat the chicken dry with paper towels.
In a small bowl, mix together the salt, black pepper, dried thyme, paprika, and garlic powder.
Rub the spice mixture all over the chicken, ensuring it is evenly coated.
Set your Instant Pot to "Sauté" mode and add the vegetable oil. Heat the oil until shimmering.
Carefully place the seasoned chicken into the Instant Pot, breast side down, and sear it for about 4-5 minutes until browned. Use tongs to flip the chicken and sear the other side for an additional 4-5 minutes.
Remove the chicken from the Instant Pot and set it aside on a plate.
Pour the chicken broth into the Instant Pot and use a wooden spoon to scrape any browned bits from the bottom of the pot. This will add flavor to the cooking liquid.
Place the trivet that came with your Instant Pot into the pot, and set the chicken on top of the trivet, breast side up. This will prevent the chicken from sitting in the liquid.
Squeeze the juice of the lemon over the chicken, and place the lemon slices inside the chicken cavity.
Close the Instant Pot lid and set the valve to the sealing position.
Select the "Manual" or "Pressure Cook" setting and set the cooking time to 6 minutes per pound of chicken.
Once the cooking time is complete, allow a natural pressure release for 10 minutes, then manually release any remaining pressure.
Carefully open the Instant Pot lid and use a meat thermometer to check the internal temperature of the chicken. It should read 165°F (74°C) in the thickest part of the thigh and the juices should run clear.
Transfer the cooked chicken to a cutting board and let it rest for a few minutes before carving.
Serve the Instant Pot whole chicken with the cooking juices and garnish with fresh herbs, if desired.
Enjoy your flavorful and tender Instant Pot whole chicken!

Instant Pot Pork Tenderloin

Ingredients:

2 pounds pork tenderloin
1 tablespoon vegetable oil
1 teaspoon salt
1/2 teaspoon black pepper
1 teaspoon dried thyme
1 teaspoon garlic powder
1 cup chicken broth or stock
1/4 cup soy sauce
2 tablespoons honey or maple syrup
2 tablespoons Dijon mustard
2 cloves garlic, minced
1 tablespoon cornstarch (optional, for thickening)

Instructions:

In a small bowl, mix together the salt, black pepper, dried thyme, and garlic powder.
Pat the pork tenderloin dry with paper towels and season it all over with the spice mixture.
Set your Instant Pot to "Sauté" mode and add the vegetable oil. Heat the oil until shimmering.
Place the seasoned pork tenderloin into the Instant Pot and sear it on all sides until browned. This will help to seal in the juices and add flavor.
In a separate bowl, whisk together the chicken broth, soy sauce, honey or maple syrup, Dijon mustard, and minced garlic.
Pour the mixture over the seared pork tenderloin in the Instant Pot.
Close the Instant Pot lid and set the valve to the sealing position.
Select the "Manual" or "Pressure Cook" setting and set the cooking time to 5 minutes per pound of pork tenderloin.
Once the cooking time is complete, allow a natural pressure release for 10 minutes, then manually release any remaining pressure.
Carefully open the Instant Pot lid and transfer the pork tenderloin to a cutting board. Let it rest for a few minutes before slicing.
If desired, you can thicken the cooking liquid into a sauce. Set the Instant Pot to "Sauté" mode again. In a small bowl, whisk together the cornstarch with a tablespoon of cold water to create a slurry. Stir the slurry into the cooking liquid in the Instant Pot and let it simmer for a few minutes until thickened.
Slice the pork tenderloin and serve it with the sauce on top.
Enjoy the tender and flavorful Instant Pot pork tenderloin with your favorite side dishes!

Instant Pot Salsa Chicken

Ingredients:

1.5 to 2 pounds boneless, skinless chicken breasts or thighs
1 cup salsa (your favorite variety)
1 teaspoon ground cumin
1 teaspoon chili powder
1/2 teaspoon garlic powder
1/2 teaspoon onion powder
1/2 teaspoon paprika
1/2 teaspoon salt
1/4 teaspoon black pepper
Optional toppings: shredded cheese, chopped cilantro, diced avocado, sour cream, lime wedges

Instructions:

Place the chicken breasts or thighs in the Instant Pot.
In a small bowl, mix together the salsa, ground cumin, chili powder, garlic powder, onion powder, paprika, salt, and black pepper. Pour the mixture over the chicken.
Close the Instant Pot lid and set the valve to the sealing position.
Select the "Manual" or "Pressure Cook" setting and set the cooking time to 8 minutes for chicken breasts or 10 minutes for chicken thighs.
Once the cooking time is complete, allow a natural pressure release for 5 minutes, then manually release any remaining pressure.
Carefully open the Instant Pot lid and use two forks to shred the chicken directly in the pot.
Give the shredded chicken a good stir to coat it with the salsa mixture.
Serve the Instant Pot salsa chicken as desired, such as in tacos, burritos, over rice, or on a salad.
Optional: Add your favorite toppings like shredded cheese, chopped cilantro, diced avocado, sour cream, or a squeeze of fresh lime juice.
Enjoy your flavorful and versatile Instant Pot salsa chicken!

Instant Pot Potatoes

Ingredients:

2 pounds potatoes (such as Yukon Gold or Russet), washed and quartered
1 cup water
1 teaspoon salt (adjust to taste)
Optional seasonings: garlic powder, onion powder, dried herbs, black pepper

Instructions:

Place the quartered potatoes in the Instant Pot insert.
Pour the water into the Instant Pot.
Sprinkle the salt and any optional seasonings over the potatoes.
Close the Instant Pot lid and set the valve to the sealing position.
Select the "Manual" or "Pressure Cook" setting and set the cooking time to 4 minutes on high pressure.
Once the cooking time is complete, do a quick pressure release by carefully turning the valve to the venting position. Be cautious of the hot steam.
Once the pressure has fully released, carefully open the Instant Pot lid.
Use a fork or a knife to check the tenderness of the potatoes. They should be easily pierced but still hold their shape.
If desired, you can transfer the cooked potatoes to a serving dish and garnish with additional herbs or seasonings.
Serve the Instant Pot potatoes as a side dish with your favorite main course.
Enjoy your perfectly cooked Instant Pot potatoes!

Instant Pot Corned Beef

Ingredients:

3-4 pounds corned beef brisket with seasoning packet
4 cups water
1 onion, quartered
4 cloves garlic, peeled and smashed
1 bay leaf
1 teaspoon black peppercorns
4 large carrots, peeled and cut into chunks
4-6 medium-sized potatoes, quartered
1 small cabbage, cut into wedges
Mustard or horseradish sauce for serving (optional)

Instructions:

Remove the corned beef from its packaging and rinse it under cold water. Pat it dry with paper towels.
Place the corned beef brisket in the Instant Pot insert. Sprinkle the included seasoning packet over the meat.
Add the water, onion, garlic, bay leaf, and black peppercorns to the Instant Pot.
Close the Instant Pot lid and set the valve to the sealing position.
Select the "Manual" or "Pressure Cook" setting and set the cooking time to 90 minutes on high pressure.
Once the cooking time is complete, allow a natural pressure release for about 10-15 minutes, then manually release any remaining pressure.
Carefully open the Instant Pot lid and remove the corned beef. Place it on a cutting board and cover it with foil to keep it warm.
Add the carrots, potatoes, and cabbage to the Instant Pot. Close the lid and set the valve to the sealing position.
Select the "Manual" or "Pressure Cook" setting and set the cooking time to 4 minutes on high pressure.
Once the cooking time is complete, do a quick pressure release by carefully turning the valve to the venting position. Be cautious of the hot steam.
Carefully open the Instant Pot lid and use a slotted spoon to remove the cooked vegetables from the pot.
Slice the corned beef against the grain into thin slices.
Serve the corned beef slices with the cooked vegetables. Optionally, serve with mustard or horseradish sauce.
Enjoy your flavorful Instant Pot corned beef and vegetables!

Instant Pot Country Style Ribs

Ingredients:

2 pounds country-style pork ribs
1 teaspoon salt
1/2 teaspoon black pepper
1 teaspoon garlic powder
1 teaspoon paprika
1/2 teaspoon dried thyme
1/2 teaspoon dried rosemary
1 cup barbecue sauce
1/2 cup chicken broth or stock
1 tablespoon vegetable oil

Instructions:

In a small bowl, mix together the salt, black pepper, garlic powder, paprika, dried thyme, and dried rosemary.
Pat the country-style ribs dry with paper towels and season them all over with the spice mixture.
Set your Instant Pot to "Sauté" mode and add the vegetable oil. Heat the oil until shimmering.
Place the seasoned country-style ribs into the Instant Pot and sear them on all sides until browned. This will help to seal in the juices and add flavor.
Remove the ribs from the Instant Pot and set them aside on a plate.
Pour the chicken broth or stock into the Instant Pot and use a wooden spoon to scrape any browned bits from the bottom of the pot. This will add flavor to the cooking liquid.
Place a trivet in the Instant Pot and arrange the seared ribs on top of the trivet.
Pour the barbecue sauce over the ribs, ensuring they are coated evenly.
Close the Instant Pot lid and set the valve to the sealing position.
Select the "Manual" or "Pressure Cook" setting and set the cooking time to 25 minutes on high pressure.
Once the cooking time is complete, allow a natural pressure release for 10 minutes, then manually release any remaining pressure.
Carefully open the Instant Pot lid and transfer the ribs to a serving platter.
If desired, you can thicken the barbecue sauce in the Instant Pot. Set the Instant Pot to "Sauté" mode again and let the sauce simmer for a few minutes until it thickens to your desired consistency.
Spoon the thickened sauce over the ribs or serve it on the side.
Enjoy your tender and flavorful Instant Pot country-style ribs!

Instant Pot BBQ Chicken

Ingredients:

2 pounds boneless, skinless chicken breasts or thighs
1 cup barbecue sauce
1/4 cup chicken broth or water
1 tablespoon Worcestershire sauce
1 tablespoon honey or brown sugar
1 teaspoon smoked paprika
1/2 teaspoon garlic powder
1/2 teaspoon onion powder
1/2 teaspoon salt
1/4 teaspoon black pepper
Optional: additional barbecue sauce for serving

Instructions:

In a bowl, mix together the barbecue sauce, chicken broth or water, Worcestershire sauce, honey or brown sugar, smoked paprika, garlic powder, onion powder, salt, and black pepper.
Place the chicken breasts or thighs in the Instant Pot.
Pour the barbecue sauce mixture over the chicken, ensuring it is well-coated.
Close the Instant Pot lid and set the valve to the sealing position.
Select the "Manual" or "Pressure Cook" setting and set the cooking time to 10 minutes on high pressure for chicken breasts or 12 minutes for chicken thighs.
Once the cooking time is complete, allow a natural pressure release for 5 minutes, then manually release any remaining pressure.
Carefully open the Instant Pot lid and use a pair of tongs to transfer the cooked chicken to a cutting board. Shred the chicken using two forks.
If desired, you can return the shredded chicken to the Instant Pot and toss it with the remaining sauce to coat it evenly.
Serve the Instant Pot BBQ chicken on buns as sandwiches, over rice, or alongside your favorite side dishes.
Optionally, you can drizzle additional barbecue sauce over the shredded chicken before serving.
Enjoy your delicious and tender Instant Pot BBQ chicken!

Instant Pot Beef Stroganoff

Ingredients:

1.5 pounds beef sirloin, cut into thin strips
1 onion, finely chopped
3 cloves garlic, minced
8 ounces cremini or button mushrooms, sliced
2 tablespoons butter
1 tablespoon vegetable oil
2 tablespoons all-purpose flour
1 cup beef broth
1 tablespoon Worcestershire sauce
1 teaspoon Dijon mustard
1 cup sour cream
Salt and pepper to taste
12 ounces egg noodles or pasta of your choice, cooked according to package instructions
Fresh parsley, chopped (for garnish, optional)

Instructions:

Set your Instant Pot to "Sauté" mode and add the vegetable oil and butter. Once the butter has melted, add the beef strips and cook until browned. Remove the beef from the Instant Pot and set it aside.
In the same Instant Pot, add the chopped onion and minced garlic. Sauté for a few minutes until the onion becomes translucent.
Add the sliced mushrooms to the Instant Pot and cook until they release their moisture and start to brown.
Sprinkle the flour over the mushrooms, onions, and garlic. Stir well to coat everything evenly.
Slowly pour in the beef broth, Worcestershire sauce, and Dijon mustard. Stir continuously to prevent lumps from forming.
Return the browned beef to the Instant Pot and stir everything together.
Close the Instant Pot lid and set the valve to the sealing position.
Select the "Manual" or "Pressure Cook" setting and set the cooking time to 15 minutes on high pressure.
Once the cooking time is complete, do a quick pressure release by carefully turning the valve to the venting position. Be cautious of the hot steam.
Carefully open the Instant Pot lid and stir in the sour cream until well combined. Season with salt and pepper to taste.
Serve the beef stroganoff over cooked egg noodles or pasta. Garnish with fresh parsley, if desired.
Enjoy your creamy and flavorful Instant Pot Beef Stroganoff!

Instant Pot Chicken and Dumplings

Ingredients:

1.5 pounds boneless, skinless chicken breasts or thighs, cut into chunks
1 onion, diced
3 carrots, sliced
3 celery stalks, sliced
3 cloves garlic, minced
4 cups chicken broth
1 teaspoon dried thyme
1 bay leaf
Salt and pepper to taste
1 cup frozen peas
1/2 cup heavy cream or whole milk
2 tablespoons cornstarch (optional, for thickening)
1 package refrigerated biscuits, quartered

Instructions:

Set your Instant Pot to "Sauté" mode and add a little oil. Once the pot is hot, add the diced onion, sliced carrots, sliced celery, and minced garlic. Sauté for a few minutes until the vegetables start to soften.
Add the chicken chunks to the Instant Pot and brown them on all sides.
Pour in the chicken broth and add the dried thyme, bay leaf, salt, and pepper. Give everything a good stir.
Close the Instant Pot lid and set the valve to the sealing position.
Select the "Manual" or "Pressure Cook" setting and set the cooking time to 10 minutes on high pressure.
Once the cooking time is complete, do a quick pressure release by carefully turning the valve to the venting position. Be cautious of the hot steam.
Carefully open the Instant Pot lid and remove the chicken chunks from the pot. Shred the chicken using two forks.
Set the Instant Pot to "Sauté" mode again. Add the frozen peas and shredded chicken back into the pot. Stir in the heavy cream or whole milk.
If you prefer a thicker broth, you can create a slurry by mixing the cornstarch with a little water, then add it to the Instant Pot. Stir well to combine and thicken the broth.
Flatten the quartered biscuits slightly and drop them into the Instant Pot on top of the chicken and vegetables.
Close the Instant Pot lid again and set the valve to the sealing position.
Select the "Manual" or "Pressure Cook" setting and set the cooking time to 5 minutes on high pressure.
Once the cooking time is complete, do a natural pressure release for 5 minutes, then manually release any remaining pressure.
Carefully open the Instant Pot lid, and you'll find fluffy dumplings on top of the chicken and vegetables.
Serve the Instant Pot chicken and dumplings hot, garnished with fresh parsley if desired.
Enjoy your comforting and delicious Instant Pot Chicken and Dumplings!

Instant Pot Chicken Wings

Ingredients:

2 pounds chicken wings
1 cup water or chicken broth
1/2 cup barbecue sauce or hot sauce
(adjust to your preference)
2 tablespoons soy sauce
2 tablespoons honey or brown sugar
1 teaspoon garlic powder
1/2 teaspoon onion powder
1/2 teaspoon paprika
1/2 teaspoon salt
Optional garnish: sesame seeds, chopped green onions

Instructions:

Place the chicken wings in the Instant Pot insert.
In a bowl, mix together the water or chicken broth, barbecue sauce or hot sauce, soy sauce, honey or brown sugar, garlic powder, onion powder, paprika, and salt.
Pour the sauce mixture over the chicken wings in the Instant Pot, ensuring they are coated well.
Close the Instant Pot lid and set the valve to the sealing position.
Select the "Manual" or "Pressure Cook" setting and set the cooking time to 10 minutes on high pressure.
Once the cooking time is complete, allow a natural pressure release for 5 minutes, then manually release any remaining pressure.
Carefully open the Instant Pot lid and use a pair of tongs to transfer the cooked chicken wings to a baking sheet lined with foil or parchment paper.
Optional: Preheat your oven broiler to high. Place the baking sheet with the chicken wings under the broiler for a few minutes until they are nicely browned and crispy. Keep a close eye on them to prevent burning.
Remove the chicken wings from the oven and let them cool slightly.
If desired, you can pour the remaining sauce from the Instant Pot into a saucepan and simmer it over medium heat until it thickens to your desired consistency. Use this sauce for dipping or drizzling over the chicken wings.
Sprinkle the cooked chicken wings with sesame seeds and chopped green onions, if desired.
Serve the Instant Pot chicken wings as an appetizer or main dish. Enjoy them hot!
Note: You can also toss the cooked chicken wings in additional barbecue sauce or hot sauce before serving for extra flavor.
Enjoy your delicious and tender Instant Pot chicken wings!

Instant Pot Mashed Potatoes

Ingredients:

2 pounds potatoes (such as Russet or Yukon Gold), peeled and cut into chunks
1 cup water or chicken broth
1/2 cup milk (whole milk or 2%)
4 tablespoons unsalted butter
1/4 cup sour cream
Salt and pepper to taste
Optional toppings: chopped chives, shredded cheese, crispy bacon bits

Instructions:

Place the potato chunks in the Instant Pot insert.
Pour the water or chicken broth over the potatoes.
Close the Instant Pot lid and set the valve to the sealing position.
Select the "Manual" or "Pressure Cook" setting and set the cooking time to 8 minutes on high pressure.
Once the cooking time is complete, do a quick pressure release by carefully turning the valve to the venting position. Be cautious of the hot steam.
Carefully open the Instant Pot lid and drain any excess liquid from the potatoes.
Add the milk and butter to the Instant Pot with the potatoes.
Using a potato masher or a hand mixer, mash the potatoes until they reach your desired consistency. Add more milk if needed to achieve your preferred creaminess.
Stir in the sour cream until well combined. Season with salt and pepper to taste.
Serve the mashed potatoes hot, garnished with optional toppings such as chopped chives, shredded cheese, or crispy bacon bits.
Enjoy your creamy and flavorful Instant Pot mashed potatoes!

Instant Pot Meatloaf

Ingredients:

1.5 pounds ground beef (lean or medium)
1/2 cup breadcrumbs
1/2 cup milk
1/2 cup grated Parmesan cheese
1/4 cup finely chopped onion
2 cloves garlic, minced
2 tablespoons Worcestershire sauce
1 tablespoon Dijon mustard
1 teaspoon dried oregano
1 teaspoon dried parsley
1/2 teaspoon salt
1/4 teaspoon black pepper
2 large eggs, beaten
1/4 cup ketchup

For the glaze:

1/4 cup ketchup
2 tablespoons brown sugar
1 tablespoon Dijon mustard

Instructions:

In a large mixing bowl, combine the ground beef, breadcrumbs, milk, grated Parmesan cheese, chopped onion, minced garlic, Worcestershire sauce, Dijon mustard, dried oregano, dried parsley, salt, black pepper, and beaten eggs. Mix well using your hands or a spoon until all the ingredients are evenly combined.
Shape the meat mixture into a loaf shape and place it on a piece of aluminum foil that's been sprayed with non-stick cooking spray. This will help lift the meatloaf out of the Instant Pot after cooking.
In a small bowl, mix together the ketchup, brown sugar, and Dijon mustard to create the glaze.
Spread the glaze evenly over the top of the meatloaf.
Pour 1 cup of water into the Instant Pot insert.
Place a trivet or a steamer basket in the Instant Pot and carefully place the foil-wrapped meatloaf on top of it.
Close the Instant Pot lid and set the valve to the sealing position.
Select the "Manual" or "Pressure Cook" setting and set the cooking time to 25 minutes on high pressure.
Once the cooking time is complete, allow a natural pressure release for 10 minutes, then manually release any remaining pressure.
Carefully open the Instant Pot lid and use oven mitts or tongs to carefully lift the foil-wrapped meatloaf out of the Instant Pot.
Remove the foil from the meatloaf and transfer it to a serving platter.
Let the meatloaf rest for a few minutes before slicing and serving.
Enjoy your tasty Instant Pot meatloaf!

Instant Pot Potato Soup

Ingredients:

4 cups potatoes, peeled and diced
1 onion, diced
2 cloves garlic, minced
4 cups chicken or vegetable broth
1 cup milk (whole milk or 2%)
1/2 cup heavy cream (optional, for a creamier soup)
4 slices bacon, cooked and crumbled (optional, for garnish)
1 cup shredded cheddar cheese (optional, for garnish)
Chopped chives or green onions (optional, for garnish)
Salt and pepper to taste

Instructions:

Set your Instant Pot to "Sauté" mode and add a little oil. Once the pot is hot, add the diced onion and minced garlic. Sauté for a few minutes until the onion becomes translucent.
Add the diced potatoes to the Instant Pot and stir to combine with the onions and garlic.
Pour in the chicken or vegetable broth, ensuring that the potatoes are fully covered.
Close the Instant Pot lid and set the valve to the sealing position.
Select the "Manual" or "Pressure Cook" setting and set the cooking time to 8 minutes on high pressure.
Once the cooking time is complete, do a quick pressure release by carefully turning the valve to the venting position. Be cautious of the hot steam.
Carefully open the Instant Pot lid and use an immersion blender or a potato masher to partially blend the soup to your desired consistency. Leave some chunks of potatoes for texture.
Stir in the milk and, if using, the heavy cream. Season with salt and pepper to taste.
Set the Instant Pot to "Sauté" mode again and let the soup simmer for a few minutes to heat through.
Serve the Instant Pot potato soup hot, garnished with crumbled bacon, shredded cheddar cheese, and chopped chives or green onions, if desired.
Enjoy your delicious and creamy Instant Pot potato soup!

Instant Pot Corn on the Cob

Ingredients:

4 ears of corn, husks and silk removed
1 cup water
Salt and butter (optional, for serving)

Instructions:

Pour the water into the Instant Pot insert.
Place a steamer basket or trivet inside the Instant Pot
Stand the ears of corn upright in the Instant Pot on top of the steamer basket or trivet.
Close the Instant Pot lid and set the valve to the sealing position.
Select the "Manual" or "Pressure Cook" setting and set the cooking time to 2 minutes on high pressure.
Once the cooking time is complete, do a quick pressure release by carefully turning the valve to the venting position. Be cautious of the hot steam.
Carefully open the Instant Pot lid and use tongs to remove the corn on the cob from the Instant Pot.
Serve the Instant Pot corn on the cob hot. Optionally, season with salt and butter to taste.
Enjoy your tender and flavorful Instant Pot corn on the cob!

Instant Pot Pasta

Ingredients:

1 pound (450g) of your preferred pasta (such as penne, spaghetti, or fettuccine)
4 cups (946ml) of water or vegetable/chicken broth
1 can (14 ounces or 400g) of diced tomatoes
1 onion, finely chopped
3 cloves of garlic, minced
1 teaspoon of dried basil
1 teaspoon of dried oregano
1/2 teaspoon of red pepper flakes (optional, for a spicy kick)
Salt and pepper to taste
2 tablespoons of olive oil
Grated Parmesan cheese, for garnish (optional)
Fresh basil or parsley, chopped, for garnish (optional)

Instructions:

Set your Instant Pot to sauté mode and heat the olive oil. Add the chopped onion and minced garlic and cook until they become fragrant and translucent, about 2-3 minutes.
Add the diced tomatoes, dried basil, dried oregano, red pepper flakes (if desired), salt, and pepper to the pot. Stir well to combine.
Break the pasta in half and add it to the Instant Pot. Pour in the water or broth and give everything a gentle stir to ensure the pasta is submerged in the liquid.
Close the Instant Pot lid, set the valve to the sealing position, and select the manual or pressure cook function. Set the cooking time according to the recommended cooking time on the pasta package, usually around 6-8 minutes for al dente.
Once the cooking time is complete, perform a quick pressure release by carefully turning the valve to venting. Be cautious of the hot steam.
When the pressure has released, open the Instant Pot lid and give the pasta a thorough stir to incorporate the sauce. Taste and adjust the seasoning if needed.
Serve the pasta hot, garnished with grated Parmesan cheese and fresh basil or parsley if desired.
This Instant Pot pasta recipe is quick, easy, and delivers a flavorful dish in no time. Enjoy your meal!

Instant Pot Spaghetti Squash

Ingredients:

1 medium-sized spaghetti squash
1 cup (236ml) of water
Salt and pepper to taste
Your favorite sauce or toppings (marinara sauce, pesto, cheese, etc.)

Instructions:

Start by carefully cutting the spaghetti squash in half lengthwise. Scoop out the seeds and discard them.
Pour the water into the Instant Pot insert. Place a trivet or a steamer basket inside the pot.
Carefully place the spaghetti squash halves on the trivet or steamer basket, cut side up.
Close the Instant Pot lid and set the valve to the sealing position.
Select the manual or pressure cook function and set the cooking time to 7-9 minutes, depending on the size of your spaghetti squash. For smaller squash, cook for 7 minutes; for larger squash, cook for 9 minutes.
Once the cooking time is complete, allow for a natural pressure release for about 10 minutes. After 10 minutes, carefully turn the valve to the venting position to release any remaining pressure.
Once the pressure has released and it's safe to open the lid, remove the spaghetti squash from the Instant Pot using tongs or a fork.
Use a fork to scrape the flesh of the spaghetti squash, which will naturally separate into spaghetti-like strands. Continue scraping until you've removed all the strands.
Season the spaghetti squash with salt and pepper to taste.
Serve the spaghetti squash hot, topped with your favorite sauce or toppings, such as marinara sauce, pesto, cheese, or sautéed vegetables.
Enjoy your Instant Pot spaghetti squash, a delicious and healthy alternative to traditional pasta!

Instant Pot Ham

Ingredients:

4-5 pounds (1.8-2.3kg) bone-in ham
1 cup (236ml) water or broth
1/2 cup (120ml) maple syrup or honey (optional)
1/4 cup (60ml) Dijon mustard (optional)
1 teaspoon garlic powder
1 teaspoon onion powder
1/2 teaspoon ground black pepper
1/2 teaspoon paprika

Instructions:

Place the trivet in the Instant Pot insert and pour the water or broth into the pot.
Remove any packaging or netting from the ham, and trim off excess fat if desired.
In a small bowl, combine the maple syrup or honey, Dijon mustard, garlic powder, onion powder, black pepper, and paprika. Mix well to create a glaze.
Brush the glaze all over the ham, ensuring it's evenly coated.
Place the ham on the trivet in the Instant Pot.
Close the Instant Pot lid and set the valve to the sealing position.
Select the manual or pressure cook function and set the cooking time to 10 minutes per pound (22 minutes per kg) of ham. For example, if you have a 4-pound (1.8kg) ham, cook it for 40 minutes
Once the cooking time is complete, allow for a natural pressure release for 10-15 minutes. After that, carefully turn the valve to the venting position to release any remaining pressure.
When the pressure has released and it's safe to open the lid, carefully remove the ham from the Instant Pot and transfer it to a serving platter.
If desired, you can glaze the ham again with any remaining sauce from the Instant Pot or place it under the broiler for a few minutes to achieve a caramelized crust.
Let the ham rest for a few minutes before slicing and serving.
Enjoy your flavorful Instant Pot ham, perfect for holiday gatherings or any special occasion!

Instant Pot Applesauce

Ingredients:

6-8 medium-sized apples (any variety you prefer)
1/2 cup (120ml) water or apple cider
1 tablespoon lemon juice (optional)
2 tablespoons honey or maple syrup (optional)
1 teaspoon ground cinnamon
1/2 teaspoon ground nutmeg (optional)
1/4 teaspoon ground cloves (optional)

Instructions:

Start by peeling, coring, and roughly chopping the apples. Remove the seeds and stems.
Place the chopped apples in the Instant Pot insert.
Add the water or apple cider to the Instant Pot. If desired, add lemon juice for a tangy flavor and to prevent browning of the apples.
If you prefer a sweeter applesauce, add honey or maple syrup to the Instant Pot.
Sprinkle the ground cinnamon, ground nutmeg, and ground cloves over the apples. These spices will add warmth and enhance the flavor.
Give everything a good stir to ensure the apples are coated with the spices and sweetener.
Close the Instant Pot lid and set the valve to the sealing position.
Select the manual or pressure cook function and set the cooking time to 6 minutes.
Once the cooking time is complete, allow for a natural pressure release for about 10 minutes. After 10 minutes, carefully turn the valve to the venting position to release any remaining pressure.
When the pressure has released and it's safe to open the lid, use a potato masher or immersion blender to mash the cooked apples until you reach your desired consistency. If you prefer a chunky applesauce, mash it lightly. For a smoother texture, blend it further.
Taste the applesauce and adjust the sweetness or spices if desired. Let the applesauce cool before transferring it to jars or airtight containers for storage.
Your homemade Instant Pot applesauce is ready to enjoy! Serve it warm or chilled as a delicious and nutritious snack or accompaniment to various dishes.

Instant Pot Lentils

Ingredients:

1 cup (200g) dried lentils (any variety you prefer)
1 small onion, finely chopped
2 cloves of garlic, minced
1 carrot, diced
1 celery stalk, diced
4 cups (946ml) vegetable broth or water
1 bay leaf
1 teaspoon ground cumin
1/2 teaspoon ground coriander
1/2 teaspoon paprika
Salt and pepper to taste
Fresh herbs (such as parsley or cilantro) for garnish (optional)

Instructions:

Rinse the lentils under cold water and remove any debris or impurities. Drain them well.
Set your Instant Pot to sauté mode and heat a tablespoon of oil. Add the chopped onion, minced garlic, diced carrot, and diced celery. Sauté for 2-3 minutes until the vegetables start to soften.
Add the drained lentils, vegetable broth or water, bay leaf, ground cumin, ground coriander, paprika, salt, and pepper to the Instant Pot. Stir well to combine.
Close the Instant Pot lid and set the valve to the sealing position.
Select the manual or pressure cook function and set the cooking time to 8 minutes for regular lentils or 4 minutes for red lentils.
Once the cooking time is complete, allow for a natural pressure release for about 10 minutes. After 10 minutes, carefully turn the valve to the venting position to release any remaining pressure.
When the pressure has released and it's safe to open the lid, give the lentils a stir and taste for seasoning adjustments. Add more salt and pepper if needed.
Serve the lentils hot, garnished with fresh herbs if desired.
Instant Pot lentils are versatile and can be enjoyed as a side dish, added to salads, or used as a base for soups and stews. They are packed with protein and fiber, making them a nutritious addition to your meals.

Instant Pot Chicken Marinara

Ingredients:

4 boneless, skinless chicken breasts
1 tablespoon olive oil
1 small onion, finely chopped
3 cloves of garlic, minced
1 can (14 ounces or 400g) crushed tomatoes
1 can (14 ounces or 400g) diced tomatoes
1 teaspoon dried basil
1 teaspoon dried oregano
1/2 teaspoon dried thyme
1/2 teaspoon red pepper flakes (optional, for a spicy kick)
Salt and pepper to taste
Fresh basil leaves, chopped, for garnish (optional)
Grated Parmesan cheese, for garnish (optional)

Instructions:

Set your Instant Pot to sauté mode and heat the olive oil. Add the chopped onion and minced garlic and cook until they become fragrant and translucent, about 2-3 minutes.
Push the onion and garlic to one side of the Instant Pot and add the chicken breasts. Cook for 2-3 minutes on each side until lightly browned.
Add the crushed tomatoes, diced tomatoes (with their juice), dried basil, dried oregano, dried thyme, red pepper flakes (if desired), salt, and pepper to the Instant Pot. Stir well to combine and scrape up any browned bits from the bottom.
Close the Instant Pot lid and set the valve to the sealing position.
Select the manual or pressure cook function and set the cooking time to 8 minutes.
Once the cooking time is complete, allow for a natural pressure release for about 5 minutes. After 5 minutes, carefully turn the valve to the venting position to release any remaining pressure.
When the pressure has released and it's safe to open the lid, remove the chicken breasts from the Instant Pot and transfer them to a cutting board. Use two forks to shred the chicken.
Return the shredded chicken to the Instant Pot and stir it into the marinara sauce.
Serve the Instant Pot Chicken Marinara over cooked pasta or with crusty bread. Garnish with fresh basil leaves and grated Parmesan cheese, if desired.
Enjoy your flavorful Instant Pot Chicken Marinara, a satisfying and easy meal that's perfect for busy weeknights!

Instant Pot Teriyaki Chicken

Ingredients:

1.5 pounds (680g) boneless, skinless chicken thighs, cut into bite-sized pieces
1/2 cup (120ml) low-sodium soy sauce
1/4 cup (60ml) water
1/4 cup (60ml) honey or maple syrup
2 tablespoons rice vinegar
2 tablespoons brown sugar
2 cloves of garlic, minced
1 teaspoon grated fresh ginger
1 tablespoon cornstarch
2 tablespoons water
Optional garnish: sesame seeds, sliced green onions

Instructions:

In a bowl, whisk together the soy sauce, water, honey or maple syrup, rice vinegar, brown sugar, minced garlic, and grated ginger to make the teriyaki sauce.
Place the chicken thighs in the Instant Pot insert.
Pour the teriyaki sauce over the chicken, making sure it is well-coated.
Close the Instant Pot lid and set the valve to the sealing position.
Select the manual or pressure cook function and set the cooking time to 8 minutes.
Once the cooking time is complete, allow for a natural pressure release for about 5 minutes. After 5 minutes, carefully turn the valve to the venting position to release any remaining pressure.
When the pressure has released and it's safe to open the lid, remove the chicken from the Instant Pot and set it aside.
In a small bowl, whisk together the cornstarch and water to create a slurry.
Set the Instant Pot to sauté mode and bring the teriyaki sauce to a simmer. Gradually whisk in the cornstarch slurry and continue cooking for a few minutes until the sauce thickens.
Return the chicken to the Instant Pot and toss it in the thickened teriyaki sauce until evenly coated.
Serve the Instant Pot Teriyaki Chicken over steamed rice or with your favorite side dishes.
Garnish with sesame seeds and sliced green onions, if desired.
Enjoy your delicious and flavorful Instant Pot Teriyaki Chicken! It's a quick and easy dish that's perfect for a satisfying meal.

Honey-Balsamic Instant Pot Chicken

Ingredients:

1.5 pounds (680g) boneless, skinless chicken breasts or thighs
1/4 cup (60ml) balsamic vinegar
1/4 cup (60ml) low-sodium soy sauce
1/4 cup (60ml) honey
2 cloves of garlic, minced
1 teaspoon grated fresh ginger
1 tablespoon olive oil
Salt and pepper to taste
Optional garnish: Fresh chopped parsley or green onions

Instructions:

In a bowl, whisk together the balsamic vinegar, soy sauce, honey, minced garlic, grated ginger, olive oil, salt, and pepper.

Place the chicken breasts or thighs in the Instant Pot insert.

Pour the honey-balsamic sauce over the chicken, ensuring it is well-coated.

Close the Instant Pot lid and set the valve to the sealing position.

Select the manual or pressure cook function and set the cooking time to 8 minutes for chicken breasts or 10 minutes for chicken thighs.

Once the cooking time is complete, allow for a natural pressure release for about 5 minutes. After 5 minutes, carefully turn the valve to the venting position to release any remaining pressure.

When the pressure has released and it's safe to open the lid, remove the chicken from the Instant Pot and set it aside.

Set the Instant Pot to sauté mode and bring the sauce to a simmer. Cook the sauce for a few minutes, stirring occasionally, until it thickens and reduces slightly.

Return the chicken to the Instant Pot and toss it in the thickened sauce until evenly coated.

Serve the Honey-Balsamic Instant Pot Chicken over rice or with your favorite side dishes.

Garnish with fresh chopped parsley or sliced green onions, if desired.

Enjoy your flavorful Honey-Balsamic Instant Pot Chicken! It's a delicious and easy dish that pairs well with various sides and is sure to satisfy your taste buds.

Instant Pot Beef Ragu

Ingredients:

2 pounds (900g) beef chuck roast, cut into chunks
1 tablespoon olive oil
1 onion, finely chopped
2 carrots, diced
2 celery stalks, diced
4 cloves of garlic, minced
1 can (14 ounces or 400g) crushed tomatoes
1 can (14 ounces or 400g) diced tomatoes
1/2 cup (120ml) beef broth
1/4 cup (60ml) red wine (optional)
1 tablespoon tomato paste
2 teaspoons dried basil
2 teaspoons dried oregano
1 teaspoon dried thyme
1 bay leaf
Salt and pepper to taste
Fresh basil leaves, chopped, for garnish (optional)
Grated Parmesan cheese, for serving

Instructions:

Set your Instant Pot to sauté mode and heat the olive oil. Add the chopped onion, diced carrots, and diced celery. Sauté for 2-3 minutes until the vegetables start to soften.
Add the minced garlic and cook for another minute until fragrant.
Push the vegetables to one side of the Instant Pot and add the beef chunks. Brown the beef on all sides for about 5 minutes.
Add the crushed tomatoes, diced tomatoes (with their juice), beef broth, red wine (if using), tomato paste, dried basil, dried oregano, dried thyme, bay leaf, salt, and pepper to the Instant Pot. Stir well to combine.
Close the Instant Pot lid and set the valve to the sealing position.
Select the manual or pressure cook function and set the cooking time to 45 minutes.
Once the cooking time is complete, allow for a natural pressure release for about 10 minutes. After 10 minutes, carefully turn the valve to the venting position to release any remaining pressure.
When the pressure has released and it's safe to open the lid, remove the bay leaf from the Instant Pot.
Use two forks to shred the beef chunks into smaller pieces.
Serve the Beef Ragu over cooked pasta or with crusty bread. Garnish with fresh chopped basil leaves, if desired.
Serve with grated Parmesan cheese on top, if desired.
Enjoy your rich and flavorful Instant Pot Beef Ragu! It's a comforting and satisfying dish that's perfect for a hearty meal.

Instant Pot Chicken and Dumplings

Ingredients:

1.5 pounds (680g) boneless, skinless chicken breasts or thighs, cut into bite-sized pieces
4 cups (950ml) low-sodium chicken broth
1 cup (240ml) water
2 carrots, sliced
2 celery stalks, sliced
1 onion, diced
3 cloves of garlic, minced
2 teaspoons dried thyme
2 teaspoons dried parsley
1 bay leaf
Salt and pepper to taste
1 cup (125g) all-purpose flour
2 teaspoons baking powder
1/2 teaspoon salt
3/4 cup (180ml) milk
2 tablespoons unsalted butter, melted
Fresh parsley, chopped, for garnish (optional)

Instructions:

Place the chicken pieces, chicken broth, water, sliced carrots, sliced celery, diced onion, minced garlic, dried thyme, dried parsley, bay leaf, salt, and pepper in the Instant Pot. Stir well to combine.

Close the Instant Pot lid and set the valve to the sealing position.

Select the manual or pressure cook function and set the cooking time to 10 minutes
Once the cooking time is complete, allow for a natural pressure release for about 5 minutes. After 5 minutes, carefully turn the valve to the venting position to release any remaining pressure
When the pressure has released and it's safe to open the lid, remove the bay leaf from the Instant Pot.
In a mixing bowl, whisk together the all-purpose flour, baking powder, and salt. Add the milk and melted butter, and stir until just combined.
Set the Instant Pot to sauté mode and bring the chicken and broth mixture to a simmer.
Drop spoonfuls of the dumpling batter into the simmering broth, creating small dumplings.
Cover the Instant Pot with a glass lid or use the Instant Pot lid with the valve set to venting (not sealing).
Allow the dumplings to cook in the simmering broth for about 10-12 minutes until they are cooked through and fluffy
Serve the Instant Pot Chicken and Dumplings hot, garnished with fresh chopped parsley if desired.
Enjoy your comforting and delicious Instant Pot Chicken and Dumplings! It's a classic dish that's perfect for cozy meals and will warm you up from the inside out.

Honey Garlic Instant Pot Chicken Breasts

Ingredients:

4 boneless, skinless chicken breasts
1/4 cup (60ml) low-sodium soy sauce
1/4 cup (60ml) honey
2 tablespoons ketchup
2 tablespoons olive oil
4 cloves of garlic, minced
1 teaspoon grated fresh ginger
1/2 teaspoon dried basil
1/2 teaspoon dried oregano
Salt and pepper to taste
Optional garnish: Sesame seeds, sliced green onions

Instructions:

In a bowl, whisk together the soy sauce, honey, ketchup, olive oil, minced garlic, grated ginger, dried basil, dried oregano, salt, and pepper.
Place the chicken breasts in the Instant Pot insert.
Pour the honey garlic sauce over the chicken, making sure it is well-coated.
Close the Instant Pot lid and set the valve to the sealing position.
Select the manual or pressure cook function and set the cooking time to 8 minutes
Once the cooking time is complete, allow for a natural pressure release for about 5 minutes. After 5 minutes, carefully turn the valve to the venting position to release any remaining pressure.
When the pressure has released and it's safe to open the lid, remove the chicken from the Instant Pot and set it aside.
Set the Instant Pot to sauté mode and bring the sauce to a simmer. Cook the sauce for a few minutes, stirring occasionally, until it thickens and reduces slightly.
Return the chicken to the Instant Pot and toss it in the thickened sauce until evenly coated
Serve the Honey Garlic Instant Pot Chicken Breasts with steamed rice or your favorite side dishes. Garnish with sesame seeds and sliced green onions, if desired.
Enjoy your flavorful Honey Garlic Instant Pot Chicken Breasts! It's a delicious and easy dish that's perfect for a quick and satisfying meal.

Instant Pot Chicken Tortilla Soup

Ingredients:

1.5 pounds (680g) boneless, skinless chicken breasts or thighs
1 tablespoon olive oil
1 onion, diced
1 red bell pepper, diced
1 jalapeño pepper, seeds removed and finely chopped (optional)
3 cloves of garlic, minced
1 can (14 ounces or 400g) diced tomatoes
1 can (14 ounces or 400g) black beans, drained and rinsed
1 can (14 ounces or 400g) corn kernels, drained
4 cups (950ml) low-sodium chicken broth
1 tablespoon chili powder
1 teaspoon ground cumin
1 teaspoon dried oregano
Salt and pepper to taste
Juice of 1 lime
Tortilla chips, for serving
Optional garnish: Shredded cheese, diced avocado, chopped fresh cilantro, sour cream

Instructions:

Set your Instant Pot to sauté mode and heat the olive oil. Add the diced onion, red bell pepper, and jalapeño pepper (if using). Sauté for 2-3 minutes until the vegetables start to soften.
Add the minced garlic and cook for anther minute until fragrant.
Push the vegetables to one side of the Instant Pot and add the chicken breasts or thighs. Brown the chicken on both sides for about 2-3 minutes per side.
Add the diced tomatoes (with their juice), black beans, corn kernels, chicken broth, chili powder, ground cumin, dried oregano, salt, and pepper to the Instant Pot. Stir well to combine.
Close the Instant Pot lid and set the valve to the sealing position.
Select the manual or pressure cook function and set the cooking time to 10 minutes.
Once the cooking time is complete, allow for a natural pressure release for about 5 minutes. After 5 minutes, carefully turn the valve to the venting position to release any remaining pressure.
When the pressure has released and it's safe to open the lid, remove the chicken from the Instant Pot and shred it into smaller pieces using two forks.
Return the shredded chicken to the Instant Pot. Stir in the lime juice.
Serve the Instant Pot Chicken Tortilla Soup hot, topped with crushed tortilla chips and garnished with shredded cheese, diced avocado, chopped fresh cilantro, and sour cream if desired.
Enjoy your delicious and comforting Instant Pot Chicken Tortilla Soup! It's a flavorful and satisfying dish that's perfect for any time of the year.

Instant Pot Chicken and Rice

Ingredients:

1.5 pounds (680g) boneless, skinless chicken breasts or thighs, cut into bite-sized pieces
2 cups (400g) long-grain white rice
2.5 cups (590ml) low-sodium chicken broth
1 onion, diced
2 cloves of garlic, minced
1 teaspoon dried thyme
1 teaspoon dried oregano
1 teaspoon paprika
1/2 teaspoon turmeric
1/2 teaspoon salt
1/4 teaspoon black pepper
2 tablespoons olive oil
Optional garnish: Chopped fresh parsley or sliced green onions

Instructions:

Set your Instant Pot to sauté mode and heat the olive oil. Add the diced onion and minced garlic, and sauté for 2-3 minutes until the onions become translucent.
Add the chicken pieces to the Instant Pot and cook for about 5 minutes, stirring occasionally, until they are browned on all sides.
Add the dried thyme, dried oregano, paprika, turmeric, salt, and black pepper to the Instant Pot. Stir well to coat the chicken with the spices.
Add the white rice and chicken broth to the Instant Pot. Stir gently to combine.
Close the Instant Pot lid and set the valve to the sealing position
Select the manual or pressure cook function and set the cooking time to 10 minutes.
Once the cooking time is complete, allow for a natural pressure release for about 5 minutes. After 5 minutes, carefully turn the valve to the venting position to release any remaining pressure.
When the pressure has released and it's safe to open the lid, fluff the chicken and rice mixture with a fork.
Serve the Instant Pot Chicken and Rice hot, garnished with chopped fresh parsley or sliced green onions if desired.
Enjoy your flavorful and easy Instant Pot Chicken and Rice! It's a hearty and satisfying meal that's perfect for a quick and delicious dinner.

Instant Pot Orange Chicken

Ingredients:
For the chicken:

1.5 pounds (680g) boneless, skinless chicken breasts, cut into bite-sized pieces
1/2 cup (60g) all-purpose flour
1/4 teaspoon salt
1/4 teaspoon black pepper
2 tablespoons vegetable oil

For the sauce:

1 cup (240ml) orange juice
1/4 cup (60ml) low-sodium soy sauce
1/4 cup (60ml) honey
2 tablespoons rice vinegar
2 cloves of garlic, minced
1 tablespoon grated fresh ginger
1 tablespoon cornstarch
1 tablespoon water

For garnish:

Sesame seeds
Sliced green onions

Instructions:

In a shallow bowl, whisk together the all-purpose flour, salt, and black pepper.
Dip the chicken pieces into the flour mixture, coating them evenly.
Set your Instant Pot to sauté mode and heat the vegetable oil. Add the chicken pieces in a single layer and brown them on all sides for about 2-3 minutes per side. You may need to do this in batches to avoid overcrowding the pot.
In a separate bowl, whisk together the orange juice, soy sauce, honey, rice vinegar, minced garlic, and grated ginger.
Pour the sauce mixture over the browned chicken in the Instant Pot.
Close the Instant Pot lid and set the valve to the sealing position.
Select the manual or pressure cook function and set the cooking time to 5 minutes.
Once the cooking time is complete, allow for a natural pressure release for about 5 minutes. After 5 minutes, carefully turn the valve to the venting position to release any remaining pressure.
When the pressure has released and it's safe to open the lid, set the Instant Pot to sauté mode.
In a small bowl, whisk together the cornstarch and water to create a slurry. Add the slurry to the Instant Pot and stir well to thicken the sauce. Cook for a few minutes until the sauce has thickened to your desired consistency.
Serve the Instant Pot Orange Chicken over steamed rice or noodles. Garnish with sesame seeds and sliced green onions.
Enjoy your delicious and tangy Instant Pot Orange Chicken! It's a flavorful and satisfying dish that's perfect for a homemade takeout experience.

Instant Pot Mac and Cheese

Ingredients:

16 ounces (454g) elbow macaroni
4 cups (950ml) water
4 tablespoons (57g) unsalted butter
2 cups (480ml) milk
2 cups (200g) shredded cheddar cheese
1 cup (100g) shredded mozzarella cheese
1/2 cup (50g) grated Parmesan cheese
1/2 teaspoon mustard powder
1/2 teaspoon garlic powder
Salt and pepper to taste
Optional garnish: Chopped fresh parsley or sliced green onions

Instructions:

Place the elbow macaroni and water in the Instant Pot insert.
Close the Instant Pot lid and set the valve to the sealing position.
Select the manual or pressure cook function and set the cooking time to 4 minutes
Once the cooking time is complete, carefully do a quick pressure release by turning the valve to the venting position.
When the pressure has released and it's safe to open the lid, drain the macaroni and set it aside.
Set your Instant Pot to sauté mode and melt the butter. Stir in the milk, shredded cheddar cheese, shredded mozzarella cheese, grated Parmesan cheese, mustard powder, and garlic powder.
Stir the cheese mixture until the cheeses are melted and the sauce is smooth and creamy. This should take a few minutes.
Add the cooked macaroni back into the Instant Pot and stir well to coat the pasta with the cheese sauce. Cook for another minute or so until the macaroni is heated through.
Taste the mac and cheese and season with salt and pepper as needed.
Serve the Instant Pot Mac and Cheese hot, garnished with chopped fresh parsley or sliced green onions if desired.
Enjoy your creamy and delicious Instant Pot Mac and Cheese! It's a classic comfort food dish that's quick and easy to make in your Instant Pot.

Instant Pot Chili

Ingredients:

1.5 pounds (680g) ground beef or turkey
1 onion, diced
3 cloves of garlic, minced
1 red bell pepper, diced
1 can (14 ounces or 400g) diced tomatoes
1 can (14 ounces or 400g) kidney beans, drained and rinsed
1 can (14 ounces or 400g) black beans, drained and rinsed
2 cups (475ml) low-sodium beef or vegetable broth
2 tablespoons tomato paste
2 tablespoons chili powder
1 tablespoon ground cumin
1 teaspoon paprika
1/2 teaspoon dried oregano
1/2 teaspoon salt
1/4 teaspoon black pepper
Optional toppings: Shredded cheese, chopped green onions, sour cream, chopped fresh cilantro

Instructions:

Set your Instant Pot to sauté mode and brown the ground beef or turkey until it's cooked through. Drain any excess fat if needed.
Add the diced onion, minced garlic, and diced red bell pepper to the Instant Pot. Sauté for 2-3 minutes until the vegetables start to soften.
Add the diced tomatoes, kidney beans, black beans, beef or vegetable broth, tomato paste, chili powder, ground cumin, paprika, dried oregano, salt, and black pepper to the Instant Pot. Stir well to combine.
Close the Instant Pot lid and set the valve to the sealing position.
Select the manual or pressure cook function and set the cooking time to 10 minutes.
Once the cooking time is complete, allow for a natural pressure release for about 10 minutes. After 10 minutes, carefully turn the valve to the venting position to release any remaining pressure.
When the pressure has released and it's safe to open the lid, stir the chili well.
Serve the Instant Pot Chili hot, topped with shredded cheese, chopped green onions, sour cream, and chopped fresh cilantro if desired.
Enjoy your hearty and flavorful Instant Pot Chili! It's a comforting and satisfying dish, perfect for chilly days or anytime you're craving a delicious bowl of chili.

Instant Pot Goulash

Ingredients:

1.5 pounds (680g) beef stew meat, cut into bite-sized pieces
1 onion, diced
2 cloves of garlic, minced
1 red bell pepper, diced
2 tablespoons tomato paste
2 cups (475ml) beef broth
1 can (14 ounces or 400g) diced tomatoes
1 tablespoon paprika
1 teaspoon caraway seeds
1/2 teaspoon dried thyme
1/2 teaspoon dried oregano
1/2 teaspoon salt
1/4 teaspoon black pepper
2 tablespoons vegetable oil
8 ounces (226g) elbow macaroni or other pasta of your choice
Optional garnish: Chopped fresh parsley or sliced green onions

Instructions:

Set your Instant Pot to sauté mode and heat the vegetable oil. Add the diced onion, minced garlic, and diced red bell pepper. Sauté for 2-3 minutes until the vegetables start to soften.
Add the beef stew meat to the Instant Pot and brown it on all sides for about 4-5 minutes. This helps to enhance the flavor of the meat.
Stir in the tomato paste, paprika, caraway seeds, dried thyme, dried oregano, salt, and black pepper. Mix well to coat the meat and vegetables.
Add the beef broth and diced tomatoes (with their juice) to the Instant Pot. Stir to combine.
Close the Instant Pot lid and set the valve to the sealing position.
Select the manual or pressure cook function and set the cooking time to 20 minutes.
Once the cooking time is complete, allow for a natural pressure release for about 10 minutes. After 10 minutes, carefully turn the valve to the venting position to release any remaining pressure.
When the pressure has released and it's safe to open the lid, stir the goulash well.
Set the Instant Pot to sauté mode again and bring the mixture to a simmer. Add the elbow macaroni or other pasta of your choice and cook until the pasta is tender, stirring occasionally. This should take about 8-10 minutes.
Serve the Instant Pot Goulash hot, garnished with chopped fresh parsley or sliced green onions if desired.
Enjoy your flavorful and comforting Instant Pot Goulash! It's a delicious and satisfying dish that's perfect for a hearty meal.

Instant Pot Beef Stroganoff

Ingredients:

1.5 pounds (680g) beef sirloin, cut into thin strips
1 onion, thinly sliced
8 ounces (227g) cremini mushrooms, sliced
2 cloves of garlic, minced
1 cup (240ml) beef broth
1 cup (240ml) sour cream
2 tablespoons all-purpose flour
2 tablespoons Worcestershire sauce
1 tablespoon Dijon mustard
1 teaspoon paprika
1/2 teaspoon dried thyme
Salt and pepper to taste
2 tablespoons vegetable oil
8 ounces (227g) egg noodles or other pasta of your choice
Optional garnish: Chopped fresh parsley

Instructions:

Set your Instant Pot to sauté mode and heat the vegetable oil. Add the beef strips and cook until they are browned on all sides. This should take about 3-4 minutes. Remove the beef from the Instant Pot and set it aside.
Add the sliced onion and sliced mushrooms to the Instant Pot. Sauté for about 3-4 minutes until the vegetables start to soften.
Stir in the minced garlic, paprika, and dried thyme. Cook for an additional minute to release the flavors.
In a small bowl, whisk together the beef broth, sour cream, flour, Worcestershire sauce, and Dijon mustard until well combined.
Pour the sauce mixture into the Instant Pot, stirring well to combine with the onions and mushrooms.
Return the browned beef to the Instant Pot and stir to coat the beef with the sauce.
Close the Instant Pot lid and set the valve to the sealing position.
Select the manual or pressure cook function and set the cooking time to 15 minutes.
Once the cooking time is complete, allow for a natural pressure release for about 10 minutes. After 10 minutes, carefully turn the valve to the venting position to release any remaining pressure.
When the pressure has released and it's safe to open the lid, stir the beef stroganoff well.
Set the Instant Pot to sauté mode again and bring the mixture to a simmer. Add the egg noodles or other pasta of your choice and cook until the pasta is tender, stirring occasionally. This should take about 8-10 minutes.
Serve the Instant Pot Beef Stroganoff hot, garnished with chopped fresh parsley if desired.
Enjoy your creamy and delicious Instant Pot Beef Stroganoff! It's a classic comfort food dish that's quick and easy to make in your Instant Pot.

Instant Pot Meatballs

Ingredients:
For the meatballs:

1 pound (454g) ground beef
1/2 cup (50g) bread crumbs
1/4 cup (60ml) milk
1/4 cup (25g) grated Parmesan cheese
1/4 cup (15g) chopped fresh parsley
1/2 teaspoon garlic powder
1/2 teaspoon onion powder
1/2 teaspoon dried oregano
1/2 teaspoon salt
1/4 teaspoon black pepper
1 egg, beaten

For the sauce:

1 can (14 ounces or 400g) crushed tomatoes
1 can (14 ounces or 400g) tomato sauce
1/4 cup (60ml) tomato paste
2 cloves of garlic, minced
1 teaspoon dried basil
1 teaspoon dried oregano
1/2 teaspoon sugar
1/2 teaspoon salt
1/4 teaspoon black pepper

Instructions:

In a large bowl, combine all the ingredients for the meatballs. Mix well using your hands until all the ingredients are evenly incorporated.
Shape the mixture into meatballs, about 1 inch (2.5cm) in diameter. Set the meatballs aside.
In the Instant Pot, combine the crushed tomatoes, tomato sauce, tomato paste, minced garlic, dried basil, dried oregano, sugar, salt, and black pepper. Stir well to combine.
Gently place the meatballs into the sauce in the Instant Pot, making sure they are submerged in the sauce.
Close the Instant Pot lid and set the valve to the sealing position.
Select the manual or pressure cook function and set the cooking time to 8 minutes.
Once the cooking time is complete, allow for a natural pressure release for about 5 minutes. After 5 minutes, carefully turn the valve to the venting position to release any remaining pressure.
When the pressure has released and it's safe to open the lid, stir the meatballs and sauce gently.
Serve the Instant Pot Meatballs hot, either on their own or with cooked pasta of your choice.
Enjoy your flavorful and tender Instant Pot Meatballs! They make a delicious meal and can be served with pasta, mashed potatoes, or enjoyed in a sub sandwich.

Instant Pot Stuffed Peppers

Ingredients:

4 bell peppers (any color)
1 pound (454g) ground beef or turkey
1 small onion, diced
2 cloves of garlic, minced
1 cup (200g) cooked rice
1 can (14 ounces or 400g) diced tomatoes
1 cup (240ml) beef or vegetable broth
1 teaspoon dried oregano
1 teaspoon dried basil
1/2 teaspoon paprika
1/2 teaspoon salt
1/4 teaspoon black pepper
1 cup (100g) shredded cheese (such as cheddar or mozzarella)

Instructions:

Cut off the tops of the bell peppers and remove the seeds and membranes from the inside. Rinse the peppers and set them aside.
Set your Instant Pot to sauté mode and heat a tablespoon of oil. Add the diced onion and minced garlic, and sauté for 2-3 minutes until they start to soften.
Add the ground beef or turkey to the Instant Pot and cook until browned, breaking it up into smaller pieces with a spoon or spatula.
Drain any excess fat if needed. Add the cooked rice, diced tomatoes (with their juice), beef or vegetable broth, dried oregano, dried basil, paprika, salt, and black pepper to the Instant Pot. Stir well to combine.
Place a trivet or a steamer basket in the Instant Pot. Stand the hollowed-out bell peppers on the trivet or in the steamer basket, making sure they are stable.
Close the Instant Pot lid and set the valve to the sealing position.
Select the manual or pressure cook function and set the cooking time to 10 minutes.
Once the cooking time is complete, allow for a natural pressure release for about 5 minutes. After 5 minutes, carefully turn the valve to the venting position to release any remaining pressure.
When the pressure has released and it's safe to open the lid, carefully remove the stuffed peppers from the Instant Pot using tongs or a spatula.
Sprinkle shredded cheese on top of each stuffed pepper. You can either place the peppers under the broiler in the oven for a few minutes to melt the cheese or put the lid back on the Instant Pot and let the residual heat melt the cheese.
Serve the Instant Pot Stuffed Peppers hot, garnished with chopped fresh parsley if desired.
Enjoy your tasty and satisfying Instant Pot Stuffed Peppers! They make a nutritious and delicious meal that's sure to please.

Instant Pot Beef Stew

Ingredients:

1.5 pounds (680g) beef stew meat, cut into bite-sized pieces
1 onion, diced
2 cloves of garlic, minced
3 carrots, peeled and sliced
3 potatoes, peeled and cubed
1 cup (240ml) beef broth
1 cup (240ml) red wine (optional)
1 can (14 ounces or 400g) diced tomatoes
2 tablespoons tomato paste
2 tablespoons Worcestershire sauce
1 tablespoon all-purpose flour
1 tablespoon dried thyme
1 teaspoon paprika
1/2 teaspoon salt
1/4 teaspoon black pepper
2 tablespoons vegetable oil

Instructions:

Set your Instant Pot to sauté mode and heat the vegetable oil. Add the diced onion and minced garlic, and sauté for 2-3 minutes until they start to soften.
Add the beef stew meat to the Instant Pot and brown it on all sides for about 4-5 minutes. This helps to enhance the flavor of the meat.
In a small bowl, whisk together the beef broth, red wine (if using), tomato paste, Worcestershire sauce, all-purpose flour, dried thyme, paprika, salt, and black pepper until well combined.
Pour the sauce mixture into the Instant Pot, stirring well to coat the beef and vegetables.
Add the sliced carrots, cubed potatoes, and diced tomatoes (with their juice) to the Instant Pot. Stir well to combine.
Close the Instant Pot lid and set the valve to the sealing position.
Select the manual or pressure cook function and set the cooking time to 25 minutes.
Once the cooking time is complete, allow for a natural pressure release for about 10 minutes. After 10 minutes, carefully turn the valve to the venting position to release any remaining pressure.
When the pressure has released and it's safe to open the lid, stir the beef stew well.
Serve the Instant Pot Beef Stew hot, garnished with chopped fresh parsley if desired.
Enjoy your hearty and flavorful Instant Pot Beef Stew! It's a comforting and satisfying dish, perfect for colder days or anytime you're in the mood for a delicious stew.

Instant Pot Carnitas

Ingredients:

3 pounds (1.4kg) pork shoulder, cut into chunks
1 onion, diced
4 cloves of garlic, minced
1 teaspoon ground cumin
1 teaspoon dried oregano
1 teaspoon chili powder
1 teaspoon paprika
1/2 teaspoon salt
1/4 teaspoon black pepper
1 cup (240ml) orange juice
1/4 cup (60ml) lime juice
2 tablespoons vegetable oil

Instructions:

Set your Instant Pot to sauté mode and heat the vegetable oil. Add the diced onion and minced garlic, and sauté for 2-3 minutes until they start to soften.
In a small bowl, combine the ground cumin, dried oregano, chili powder, paprika, salt, and black pepper.
Season the pork shoulder chunks with the spice mixture, making sure to coat all sides.
Add the seasoned pork shoulder chunks to the Instant Pot and sear them on all sides for about 3-4 minutes until browned. This helps to lock in the flavors.
Pour the orange juice and lime juice over the pork shoulder in the Instant Pot.
Close the Instant Pot lid and set the valve to the sealing position.
Select the manual or pressure cook function and set the cooking time to 60 minutes.
Once the cooking time is complete, allow for a natural pressure release for about 10 minutes. After 10 minutes, carefully turn the valve to the venting position to release any remaining pressure.
When the pressure has released and it's safe to open the lid, remove the pork shoulder chunks from the Instant Pot and shred them using two forks.
Set the Instant Pot to sauté mode again and return the shredded pork to the pot. Cook for an additional 5 minutes, stirring occasionally, to crisp up the edges.
Serve the Instant Pot Carnitas hot, either as a filling for tacos, burritos, or bowls. You can also serve it with rice, beans, and you favorite toppings.
Enjoy your flavorful and tender Instant Pot Carnitas! They make a delicious and versatile dish that's perfect for gatherings or a weeknight dinner.

Instant Pot Ribs

Ingredients:

2 racks of baby back ribs
1 cup (240ml) water
1 cup (240ml) barbecue sauce
1/4 cup (60ml) apple cider vinegar
2 tablespoons brown sugar
2 teaspoons smoked paprika
1 teaspoon garlic powder
1 teaspoon onion powder
1/2 teaspoon salt

Instructions:

Remove the membrane from the back of the ribs. This will help the flavors penetrate the meat better.
In a small bowl, whisk together the barbecue sauce, apple cider vinegar, brown sugar, smoked paprika, garlic powder, onion powder, salt, and black pepper until well combined. This will be the rib sauce.
Pour the water into the Instant Pot inner pot.
Rub the rib sauce all over the racks of ribs, making sure to coat them well on all sides.
Roll up the racks of ribs and place them vertically in the Instant Pot, with the meaty side facing outward.
Close the Instant Pot lid and set the valve to the sealing position.
Select the manual or pressure cook function and set the cooking time to 25 minutes.
Once the cooking time is complete, allow for a natural pressure release for about 10 minutes. After 10 minutes, carefully turn the valve to the venting position to release any remaining pressure.
When the pressure has released and it's safe to open the lid, carefully remove the racks of ribs from the Instant Pot and place them on a baking sheet lined with aluminum foil.
Brush the ribs with additional barbecue sauce from the Instant Pot.
Preheat your oven broiler on high. Place the baking sheet with the ribs under the broiler for about 3-5 minutes until the sauce caramelizes and the ribs develop a nice glaze. Keep a close eye on them to prevent burning.
Remove the ribs from the oven and let them rest for a few minutes before cutting into individual ribs.
Serve the Instant Pot Ribs hot, with extra barbecue sauce on the side if desired.
Enjoy your tender and flavorful Instant Pot Ribs! They make a fantastic meal for BBQ lovers and are great for parties or family gatherings.

Instant Pot Minestrone Soup

Ingredients:

2 tablespoons olive oil
1 onion, diced
2 carrots, diced
2 celery stalks, diced
3 cloves of garlic, minced
1 zucchini, diced
1 cup (180g) diced tomatoes (canned or fresh)
1 can (14 ounces or 400g) kidney beans, drained and rinsed
1 can (14 ounces or 400g) cannellini beans, drained and rinsed
4 cups (960ml) vegetable broth
1 cup (240ml) water
1 teaspoon dried oregano
1 teaspoon dried basil
1/2 teaspoon dried thyme
1/2 teaspoon salt
1/4 teaspoon black pepper
1 cup (100g) small pasta (such as ditalini or macaroni)
Freshly grated Parmesan cheese, for serving
Chopped fresh parsley, for garnish

Instructions:

Set your Instant Pot to sauté mode and heat the olive oil. Add the diced onion, carrots, celery, and minced garlic, and sauté for 3-4 minutes until they start to soften.
Add the diced zucchini, diced tomatoes, kidney beans, cannellini beans, vegetable broth, water, dried oregano, dried basil, dried thyme, salt, and black pepper to the Instant Pot. Stir well to combine.
Close the Instant Pot lid and set the valve to the sealing position.
Select the manual or pressure cook function and set the cooking time to 8 minutes.
Once the cooking time is complete, allow for a natural pressure release for about 5 minutes. After 5 minutes, carefully turn the valve to the venting position to release any remaining pressure.
When the pressure has released and it's safe to open the lid, add the small pasta to the Instant Pot.
Set the Instant Pot to sauté mode again and cook the soup for an additional 5-6 minutes until the pasta is cooked to your desired tenderness, stirring occasionally.
Serve the Instant Pot Minestrone Soup hot, garnished with freshly grated Parmesan cheese and chopped fresh parsley.
Enjoy your delicious and comforting Instant Pot Minestrone Soup! It's a hearty and nutritious dish that's perfect for chilly days or anytime you're in the mood for a flavorful soup.

Instant Pot Butternut Squash Soup

Ingredients:

1 medium butternut squash, peeled, seeded, and cubed
1 onion, diced
2 cloves of garlic, minced
2 carrots, diced
1 apple, peeled, cored, and diced
4 cups (960ml) vegetable broth
1/2 teaspoon ground cinnamon
1/4 teaspoon ground nutmeg
1/4 teaspoon ground ginger
1/4 teaspoon ground cayenne pepper (optional, for a spicy kick)
Salt and pepper, to taste
1/2 cup (120ml) coconut milk or heavy cream (optional, for added creaminess)
Chopped fresh parsley or cilantro, for garnish

Instructions:

Set your Instant Pot to sauté mode and add a tablespoon of oil. Once heated, add the diced onion and minced garlic. Sauté for 2-3 minutes until the onions become translucent.

Add the cubed butternut squash, diced carrots, diced apple, vegetable broth, ground cinnamon, ground nutmeg, ground ginger, and ground cayenne pepper (if using) to the Instant Pot. Stir well to combine.

Close the Instant Pot lid and set the valve to the sealing position.

Select the manual or pressure cook function and set the cooking time to 8 minutes.

Once the cooking time is complete, allow for a natural pressure release for about 10 minutes. After 10 minutes, carefully turn the valve to the venting position to release any remaining pressure.
When the pressure has released and it's safe to open the lid, use an immersion blender to puree the soup until smooth. Alternatively, you can transfer the soup to a blender in batches and blend until smooth, then return it to the Instant Pot.
Season the soup with salt and pepper to taste. If desired, stir in the coconut milk or heavy cream for added creaminess.
Set the Instant Pot to sauté mode again and heat the soup for a few minutes until warmed through.
Serve the Instant Pot Butternut Squash Soup hot, garnished with chopped fresh parsley or cilantro.
Enjoy your warm and comforting Instant Pot Butternut Squash Soup! It's a delicious and nutritious soup that's perfect for cozy evenings or as a starter for a special meal.

Instant Pot Vegetable Soup

Ingredients:

1 tablespoon olive oil
1 onion, diced
2 cloves of garlic, minced
2 carrots, diced
2 celery stalks, diced
1 bell pepper, diced
1 zucchini, diced
1 cup (150g) diced tomatoes (canned or fresh)
4 cups (960ml) vegetable broth
1 teaspoon dried thyme
1 teaspoon dried basil
1/2 teaspoon dried oregano
1/2 teaspoon paprika
1/2 teaspoon salt
1/4 teaspoon black pepper
2 cups (300g) diced potatoes
1 cup (150g) frozen corn kernels
1 cup (150g) frozen green peas
Fresh parsley, for garnish (optional)

Instructions:

Set your Instant Pot to sauté mode and heat the olive oil. Add the diced onion and minced garlic, and sauté for 2-3 minutes until they start to soften.
Add the diced carrots, diced celery, diced bell pepper, and diced zucchini to the Instant Pot. Sauté for an additional 3-4 minutes until the vegetables start to soften.
Add the diced tomatoes, vegetable broth, dried thyme, dried basil, dried oregano, paprika, salt, and black pepper to the Instant Pot. Stir well to combine.
Add the diced potatoes, frozen corn kernels, and frozen green peas to the Instant Pot. Stir well to distribute the ingredients evenly.
Close the Instant Pot lid and set the valve to the sealing position.
Select the manual or pressure cook function and set the cooking time to 5 minutes.
Once the cooking time is complete, allow for a natural pressure release for about 5 minutes. After 5 minutes, carefully turn the valve to the venting position to release any remaining pressure.
When the pressure has released and it's safe to open the lid, give the soup a stir.
Serve the Instant Pot Vegetable Soup hot, garnished with fresh parsley if desired.
Enjoy your delicious and nutritious Instant Pot Vegetable Soup! It's a comforting and flavorful dish that's packed with a variety of vegetables. Perfect for a light lunch or dinner.

Instant Pot Steel Cut Oats

Ingredients:

1 cup steel cut oats
3 cups water
1 cup milk (dairy or plant-based)
1 tablespoon butter or coconut oil (optional)
1 teaspoon vanilla extract
Pinch of salt
Optional toppings: fresh fruits, nuts, seeds, honey, maple syrup, cinnamon, etc.

Instructions:

Rinse the steel cut oats under cold water and drain.
Add the rinsed steel cut oats, water, milk, butter or coconut oil (if using), vanilla extract, and salt to the Instant Pot.
Close the Instant Pot lid and set the valve to the sealing position.
Select the manual or pressure cook function and set the cooking time to 4 minutes.
Once the cooking time is complete, allow for a natural pressure release for about 10 minutes. After 10 minutes, carefully turn the valve to the venting position to release any remaining pressure.
When the pressure has released and it's safe to open the lid, give the oats a good stir.
Serve the Instant Pot Steel Cut Oats hot, topped with your favorite toppings such as fresh fruits, nuts, seeds, honey, maple syrup, or a sprinkle of cinnamon.
Enjoy your warm and creamy Instant Pot Steel Cut Oats! They make a wholesome and satisfying breakfast to start your day off right. Feel free to adjust the sweetness and toppings according to your preference.

Instant Pot Brown Rice

Ingredients:

1 cup brown rice
1 ¼ cups water
1 tablespoon oil or butter (optional)
½ teaspoon salt (optional)

Instructions:

Rinse the brown rice under cold water and drain.
Add the rinsed brown rice, water, oil or butter (if using), and salt (if using) to the Instant Pot.
Close the Instant Pot lid and set the valve to the sealing position.
Select the manual or pressure cook function and set the cooking time to 22 minutes.
Once the cooking time is complete, allow for a natural pressure release for about 10 minutes.
After 10 minutes, carefully turn the valve to the venting position to release any remaining pressure.
When the pressure has released and it's safe to open the lid, fluff the rice with a fork.
Serve the Instant Pot Brown Rice as a side dish or as a base for your favorite stir-fries, curries, or other dishes.
Enjoy your perfectly cooked Instant Pot Brown Rice! It's a nutritious and versatile grain that pairs well with a variety of dishes. Feel free to adjust the cooking time slightly based on your preference for softer or firmer rice.

Instant Pot Carbonara Pasta

Ingredients:

8 ounces (225g) spaghetti or fettuccine pasta
4 slices bacon, chopped
3 cloves garlic, minced
2 large eggs
1/2 cup (120ml) heavy cream
1/2 cup (50g) grated Parmesan cheese
Salt and pepper, to taste
Chopped fresh parsley, for garnish (optional)

Instructions:

Break the spaghetti or fettuccine pasta in half and place it in the Instant Pot. Add enough water to cover the pasta, about 4 cups (960ml). Add a pinch of salt.
Close the Instant Pot lid and set the valve to the sealing position.
Select the manual or pressure cook function and set the cooking time to half the time stated on the pasta package instructions. For example, if the package instructions say to cook the pasta for 10 minutes, set the Instant Pot cooking time to 5 minutes.
Once the cooking time is complete, do a quick pressure release by carefully turning the valve to the venting position.
When the pressure has released and it's safe to open the lid, drain the pasta and set it aside.
Set the Instant Pot to sauté mode and add the chopped bacon. Cook the bacon until crispy, stirring occasionally.
Add the minced garlic to the Instant Pot with the crispy bacon and sauté for about 1 minute until fragrant.
In a separate bowl, whisk together the eggs, heavy cream, and grated Parmesan cheese.
Pour the egg mixture into the Instant Pot with the bacon and garlic. Stir well to combine.
Add the cooked and drained pasta back into the Instant Pot. Stir until the pasta is coated with the creamy sauce.
Cook the pasta in the Instant Pot on sauté mode for an additional 1-2 minutes, stirring constantly, until the sauce thickens slightly and coats the pasta.
Season with salt and pepper to taste.
Serve the Instant Pot Carbonara Pasta hot, garnished with chopped fresh parsley if desired.
Enjoy your creamy and flavorful Instant Pot Carbonara Pasta! It's a quick and satisfying meal that's perfect for busy weeknights. Adjust the seasonings and add any additional ingredients, such as peas or mushrooms, to personalize your carbonara pasta.

I want to take a moment to express my heartfelt gratitude for your recent purchase of my recipe book. As a passionate food lover, nothing makes me happier than sharing my favorite recipes with others. Your decision to invest in my book not only supports my dream, but also shows your commitment to expanding your culinary horizons.

I sincerely hope that the recipes in the book will inspire you to try new things and add some excitement to your meals.

Thank you again for your support and for being a part of this journey with me. I hope my book will bring you many happy and delicious moments in the kitchen.

www.ingramcontent.com/pod-product-compliance
Lightning Source LLC
Chambersburg PA
CBHW081236080526
44587CB00022B/3963